H TO START A CULT

JODY RAYNSFORD

www.get-known.co.uk

CONTENTS

HOW TO START A CULT IS A...

**NO.1 AMAZON BEST SELLER
MARKETING & SALES**

**NO.1 AMAZON BEST SELLER
SMALL BUSINESS**

**NO.1 AMAZON BEST SELLER
BRANDS & CORPORATE IDENTITY**

Before you read this book, I want to show you that building a cult really does work.

Ahead of the book's release, I set a goal of being Christmas No.1 in the Amazon charts (move over, Cliff...)

It seemed like a crazy idea to everyone involved but I wanted to do a test that would help sell the book and the ideas in the book.

Could I launch the book solely to a cult audience (and no-one else) and get it to No.1 without any marketing?

A book launch without a promotional campaign? Surely, that was doomed to fail. If you were doing this the traditional way, it would.

But this is the way of the cult. And as you can see at the start of this mini chapter, the launch was pretty successful.

So basically, I proved the value and method of starting a cult by getting my cult to buy a book about starting cults in sufficient numbers to reach Christmas number one. So if you were wondering who am I to talk about cults, there's your answer.

Got it? Great.

On with the book...

WHAT ARE YOU DOING HERE?

You can tell a lot about a person by their choice of literature.

I mean, seriously– what kind of person picks up a book called *How to Start a Cult*?

You've decided to go full-blown cult...

And I like that in you because it says a lot about how you think.

You don't want customers.

Or 'fans'.

Or a 'tribe'.

Or any half-arsed, wishy-washy guff like that.

You want dead-on, devoted, stamp-me-with-a-tattoo-and-tell-me-my-next-mission, Project Mayhem-style cult followers.

And who wouldn't?

If that sounds like you, you're my kind of gal/guy/non-gender-specific equivalent. We're going to get on like a house on fire.

If this terrifies you, it seems like you've made a dreadful mistake wandering in here; I suggest putting this book down right now and choosing something a bit more palatable for your delicate tastes. Maybe something by Jay Shetty with a bunch of stolen motivational quotes.

THIS BOOK IS REALLY NOT FOR YOU IF...

- You're looking for a quick fix to solve your problems. My approach takes courage and effort to set up but brings consistent, long-term results.

- You're collapsing under a ton of customer complaints, product recalls and refunds, and you want it to stop. You're going to need a solid product or service for me to be able to help you.

- You're into self-help/business book porn and you're only reading this so you can slap a photo of the cover on Instagram to show your followers what a clever person you are (pat on the head for you).

- You're forever in the planning stage and never get anything done. This revolution needs action-takers, not posers.

- You're scared shitless of saying or doing anything that may offend/upset/irritate anyone (this is cult-building, goddamn it – what did you expect?).

If any of those sounds like you, turn back now. There's no shame in it, seriously. It's better you don't waste your time on these pages, because we're not going to be a good fit.

As Obi-Wan would say with a wave of his hand: 'This isn't the strategy you're looking for.'

Something else will probably work for you. But not this.

So, close this book. Put it back on the shelf, leave it for someone it will appeal to, and off you trot.

OK. They're gone now. Let's get down to business.

THIS BOOK IS FOR YOU IF...

If you're still here, then let me guess: you've been in business a while and kicked ass in the past, but it kinda feels like you've lost your way a bit. You find yourself wondering why your people and customers aren't as excited about what you do as they used to be – and, if you're honest, why you aren't either. You know something has to be done before you stagnate – or worse, shrink – especially because every time you look over your shoulder, a new challenger brand has popped up.

I'd wager the following are keeping you up at night:

- Sales growth has plateaued, your sales team is struggling to win pitches, and you don't know why.

- You're anxious your competition is gnawing away at

your market share, and wondering why your customers don't love you like they used to.

- Your brand or product is not even close to getting the attention it deserves, while newcomers snapping at your heels seem to draw media coverage like moths to a flame.

- You're worried about keeping your team together, watching talent slip away and the team's morale spiral downwards.

- You just can't strike a decisive blow in your market that fires you ahead of everyone else.

- You're concerned that everything you've built up is at risk of falling apart.

- Everything feels like a struggle right now. Sales are harder. Hiring is harder. And growing the business feels like a slog.

- You're feeling frustrated, anxious and paralysed, not knowing what your next move should be.

THIS BOOK WILL...

If that sounds like you, I get it. I've been there myself and that's why I can help you. Because if you follow what I show you in this book, here's what happens.

First, your brand becomes magnetic, effortlessly attracting the right customers, staff and media attention. Customers truly love you and spread your word like gospel. I mean it – your devotees will be devout.

Second, your competition becomes irrelevant. They'll be left wondering what the hell hit them.

Third, the love from your customers will be so strong that you won't be left vulnerable to massive market shocks. You won't crumble when the next pandemic hits. You'll be rock solid.

Once that happens, everything gets easier. The business will get back on track, and you'll fall back in love with it. You'll grow in a sustainable, reliable way. You'll also feel more confident in who you are, your message and your story, and customers will pick up on that.

All this from starting a cult? Seriously? Sounds too good to be true, I know. But I'll show you how through the medium of this weighty tome (less weighty, of course, if you're reading this on a Kindle).

So, here's my promise to you. Dedicate the time you need to read this book and you will:

- Discover why you're marketing your business and brand using outdated principles and ideas that no longer work, and why you need to fix that as a matter of urgency.

- Understand how the business landscape has changed and why all the strategies that used to work are dead in the water.

- Extract what your brand can learn from cults and cult leaders (and I'm not talking the weird sex and alien stuff – that's a different book).

- Learn a bulletproof method to start your own cult so that you can build belonging, become magnetic and get momentum behind your brand.

- And if you REALLY want to accelerate what you'll learn in this book and build a cult-like following for your brand you can register for the free 'How to Start a Cult' mini course at **www.cultbrandmethod.com**

WHY CULTS?

Let's deal with the Charles Manson–shaped elephant in the room. Cults don't exactly have a great reputation; I mean, it's not the most obvious model for the future of your brand wanting to follow in the footsteps of the Heaven's Gate cult or any number of strange sects that emerge around the world.

But if we can separate the good from the bad, you can take something really powerful from what cults do well. It is possible to draw positive learnings from cult leaders without getting all weird about it.

I mean, think about it – why would anyone actively want to join a cult?

Throughout history, cults have successfully brought followers together behind an enigmatic leader or cause; these followers will say, do and think what they are directed to do, all in the name of the cause.

The worst cults are centred on their leaders and a strict adherence to doctrine; they create a singular path to redemption and encourage zero critical thought, with followers taught not to question the leader or their teachings. I think we can objectively agree that is bad. (If you're umming and ahhing at this point, you need to take a long, hard look at yourself in the mirror.)

But every cult also knows exactly how to attract and indoctrinate new devotees, and keep them within its walls. When it turns pathological, cult worship becomes sinister.

The question is how we can use some of these lessons to replicate this in our own business, community or cause, and engender the same loyalty, belonging and following without any creepiness.

I genuinely believe that the world needs more cults. We need more leaders, like you, to step up and grow their own bands of belonging. Coming together is the path to solving so many of our issues.

When companies, communities and organisations build cult brands, they serve their customers better, bring more care to the world, engender greater belonging and reduce loneliness and isolation.

Building cults isn't just great for our well-being; it's great for business, too. Our sense of identity is directly connected to a feeling of belonging. And when someone feels aligned and enhanced by associating with you, your brand or your cult following, they will do anything for you. That sounds incredibly manipulative when I put it down on paper. But what it actually translates to is real following and connection.

Good businesses don't always build great brands, and that's down to how they think about their customers, followers and fans. It's my mission to show you how to bring more colour, belonging and humour to the world in the form of your own cult. Together, through building our own cults, we're going to change the world for the better. So let's get started.

Now, I don't want you to read this and start using what you learn for evil purposes. We've got enough douchebags in positions of power without adding more pathological personality cults to the mix (even as lovely a personality as I'm sure yours is…).

With this in mind, I want you to hold your left hand in the air and read out the following commitment before you read on. It is imperative you do this.

I, (say your name) hereby promise

that what I'm about to read

I will not use for evil or nefarious purposes,

to manipulate others or cause pain,

to start weird alien or sex cults,

or elect right-wing bigots to positions of authority.

And even if I do, I will be 100% responsible for my own actions, and liability will rest with myself and solely with myself and not with Jody Raynsford or any of Jody Raynsford's companies.

So help me God/Allah/Yahweh/Buddha/Ryan Reynolds (delete as appropriate).

Done? Now turn over the page…

Did you read it out loud and hold your left hand in the air?

Really?

No?

I gave you one job. That was all you had to do.

Consider why you thought it didn't apply to you. Think you're special, huh?

This could be harder than I thought. You're showing a serious lack of self-discipline.

If you skipped it, grab a pen, go back and sign it.

Don't get cocky. There are plenty more booby traps along the way if you don't keep your eyes peeled.

For now, let's talk about why you need me to get your arse in gear.

WHY ACCEPT ME AS YOUR LEADER?

I have:

- Helped brands of all sizes in a range of sectors to succeed by being bold and different

- Written and launched promotions that have sold millions of dollars' worth of products in the US and UK

- Spoken on the topics of branding, marketing and differentiation at events

- Taught over 1,000 businesses, brands and entrepreneurs how to nail their message and story

- Successfully launched and grown three separate brands

- Founded and co-hosted an award-winning podcast.

Oh, and I accidentally started a cult…

PART 1

SO YOU WANT TO START A CULT?

BRAND LOYALTY IS DEAD

You're not going to like this chapter. In fact, you're going to hate what I have to say, for one reason: once you read it, you'll know you're going to have to do something different. That means stepping outside your comfort zone. Changing something. Feeling that pang of worry that you're in uncharted territory and you have no idea of your destination.

If you're like 99% of business owners, entrepreneurs and leaders, you're going to want to retreat from what I'm about to tell you. That's fine. In fact, it's probably best if you stop right here, close this book and go back to doing exactly what you were doing before.

I mean, you'll probably be out of business in the next 5–10 years if you don't change, but at least you won't have lots of hurt feelings that come from sticking your head above the parapet and standing out. Let's be honest: more likely than not, you're in that group. There's nothing wrong with that, but the rest of this book probably isn't for you.

This is the last warning before you continue, and I can't be held responsible for your actions after this point (it's also worth noting that by throwing this book across the room, you will likely knock about 30% off the Amazon Marketplace value when you come to get rid. Best gift it to a friend or colleague who has the balls to do something with it. I won't make any profit, but at least I'll know that someone with the cojones to take action is reading these words).

If you have decided to push on, you're either:

a)   Someone who knows that what they're doing right now isn't going to grow their business and make them stand out as the go-to brand in their sector, leaving their competition in the dust, or

b)   Someone who is kidding themselves they're an a).

Even if you're a b), I'm going to show you how you can become an a).

OK, so now we've cleared that up, let me hit you with it: brand loyalty is dead.

The golden age of winning customers to your brand so they love you and endlessly buy from you without a moment's thought is no more. If that era were a bird, it would be – in the words of Monty Python – an ex-parrot.

All those customers you've been spending thousands of pounds/dollars on attracting, and all those products you've sold, don't mean diddly in the face of the new landscape.

The fact is, you're now competing in the toughest market that ever existed. Forget about the marketing messages your customer is being bombarded by. Their lives have never been busier or more full of distraction. As I show you later in this book, you're not competing against other brands in your market for your future customers' attention – you're competing against all the other things going on in their lives. Your brand versus their kids. I don't care how great your brand is; that is one battle you're not going to win. But you can become a part of their lives in a different way.

But, I hear you retort:

- 'Our customers love us – they keep coming back.'

- 'We've sold a load of products!'

- 'Look at all our five-star reviews!'

Look, there's no doubt you've got where you are by delivering what you say you deliver well. It's just… the game has changed.

"

The truth is that if
you compete on price,
service or convenience,
you're already dead

In an age where you can buy anything you want from anywhere in the world at the click of a button and get it just as quickly, you're going to have to do something pretty spectacular to even just survive the sharks circling you.

The truth is that if you compete on price, service or convenience, you're already dead. Someone *is* going to usurp you. In fact, they probably already have.

Deep down, you may already sense that the market is getting tougher. As the leader of an established business, you'll probably know that things have shifted. The landscape moved almost imperceptibly at the start, but is now heading in a direction that has you worried. Why else would you be reading this book?

You cannot afford to look away from reality any more. You know you're headed in only one direction when:

- Your marketing isn't working as well as it used to.

- Leads are drying up.

- Customers are slipping away.

- You're losing more pitches than you're winning.

- Your competitors are getting more media attention than you.

- New entrants to your market are catching you up.

And it's likely even having an effect on your team: hiring talent is harder, retaining staff is a problem, your culture is shaky at best and there's an overall sense that the trajectory is very much pointed downwards.

You're more likely at some kind of crossroads in your business. You've grown it to the point where you're now facing a choice. Do you take it to the level you always knew it could reach? Or do you keep battling it out in the arena with all the other businesses, knowing the fight has got a lot harder?

You (hopefully) have a good product or service which you've successfully sold to your audience. Now your focus is on extending your brand, reaching out to new followers and customers, and building a stronger relationship with your existing audience and customer base.

This is the point where I switch from being a bit of an asshole to laying a sympathetic hand on your shoulder and telling you that everything will be OK, that there's nothing wrong with your business, that it's not your fault and that we can get through this.

Well, here's the bad news: it is completely your fault.

But here's the good news: it is completely your fault.

As a leader you have the power to change this situation and transform your business. I will show you exactly how to grow your business on a solid foundation that not only bonds your customers to you – in place of brand loyalty – but effortlessly attracts those with whom you want to do business. More than that, the tactics in this book will provide direction and purpose to your team and I have no doubt will re-energise your love for your business.

Fallen out of love with your business? What I show you in this book will rekindle that fire and get you back in the mood again.

Most businesses tackle a plateau or a struggle to grow with the wrong strategy. Instead of realising they need a different approach, they look backwards. They double down on what they are already doing, throwing even more cash, time and effort at an approach that no longer works. It's a waste.

Sure, if you're one of those big, dumb start-ups with $100 million to burn through every week, you've probably got enough time and resource to lurch from idea to idea until, through trial and error, you eventually find your way. (I'm guessing that's not you. But if it is, shame on you blowing all that cash!)

Even if that does help you to survive in the short term, it's not an approach that solves your underlying problems and gets you where you want to be. You're just kicking the can down the road for a few months.

You can choose to face reality and deal with it now. But no amount of cash will help if you don't focus on the right things.

THE REAL REASON YOU'RE STRUGGLING

If you're wondering why what you did before isn't working now, here it is. It comes down to this sucker-punch:

No one cares about your brand.

There, I said it. Given all the hard work you've put in and how far you've come, that may come as a bit of a hammer blow. But the sooner you face up to this reality, the greater the advantage you have over everyone else who still has their head stuck in the sand.

It's really important to understand and believe this point before we move on. You may still be labouring under the misapprehension that your current customers or clients are buying from you because of a sense of real connection with you or your brand. But when you get under the skin of that assumption, just how sure are you that they wouldn't scarper to the next sexy brand that flutters its eyelids at them and offers them exactly what you do at 20% of the cost?

Be honest with yourself right now. All things being equal, are you confident your customers and clients would stick with you? Or would the majority abandon you quicker than the BBC would abandon a *Blue Peter* presenter with a coke problem?

It would take someone with a highly optimistic view of their brand to stress-test their customers' loyalty in this way.

This begs the question: if customers don't care about your brand, what do they care about?

As I've already mentioned, you're competing for attention. The best way to grab and keep someone's attention is to reach them on an emotional level, and there is no subject they love to think more deeply about than themselves.

That's not a judgement on people being selfish or self-centred. It's just human. We think from our own perspective. We view the world through the lens of our own thoughts and feelings. Our internal dictates our external. What we feel translates to what we do – and, ultimately, what we choose to spend our time and money on.

To truly reach and connect with anyone in a meaningful way, you have to do more than just appeal to their rational thoughts; you have to make them feel something. People connect with how you make them feel on an emotional level. That connection will always be stronger than 'brand loyalty'.

What we're ultimately talking about is a force that can move people to do things they wouldn't otherwise do, inspire them to action and, most importantly, feel good about themselves.

That force is *belonging*.

Instead of focusing on the transient nature of 'brand loyalty', those few brands that concentrate on developing a genuine sense of belonging with their audience are more resilient. They can withstand market fluctuations, recessions and even global pandemics. They stand head and shoulders above their competitors. They thrive while others collapse. And they do it because they're not playing in the same ballpark.

HOW I ACCIDENTALLY STARTED A CULT

I t was an accident.

That's all I can say.

What started off as two ordinary chaps having a casual conversation in their living rooms over Skype five years ago transformed into something we never expected.

Thousands of runners in races across the world wearing our quotes, performing bizarre acts of devotion, winning awards and being invited to host events. And the pièce de résistance: the extremely worrying sight of one of our 'fans' getting our slogan tattooed on their leg.

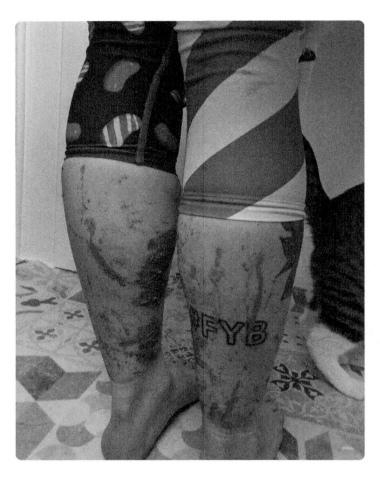

This is definitely not what we expected.

*The community was
self-perpetuating with user-
generated content within days
of being launched and has
remained this way since*

of this was that the community sounded NOTHING like any other running group on Facebook– and there are tons of them, all navel-gazing and boasting about their times or asking each other for dull shoe recommendations. The BBR community felt completely different, far more engaged and a natural extension to the podcast. We talked about failure, our worst or strangest experiences, what pants to wear, the joy of giving up or having a tantrum mid-ultra – all the post-race pub chat that real people had. And here's a fact that anyone who has run a podcast group won't believe: since launch, we have never had to add a single piece of content in the group to keep the conversation going and keep people engaged. The community was self-perpetuating with user-generated content within days of being launched and has remained this way since. Amazing, I know.

The community and podcast grew together. And here's the important thing: the numbers weren't massive. We're not talking about millions of subscribers and hundreds or even tens of thousands in the Facebook group. With fewer than a thousand members, we had a deeper and richer experience with our own tribe.

Now that we had more of a connection with our community and could hear directly from them, we used that on the podcast. Feedback was more immediate and clearer – and while we stuck to our guns around what we were about, we listened to what our fans told us.

BREAKING OUR OWN RULES

'We will NEVER release episodes longer than 30 minutes because who the hell has time for that?' we proclaimed on one of our first episodes. The idea was to keep them short and sharp so they were a quick and easy listen. That lasted six months.

The community told us they wanted more content. We upped the episodes from around 20 minutes each to some that lasted three hours or more. The reason this worked was that people wanted to listen to us on their long weekend runs or in the car driving or commuting, and 20 minutes just wasn't enough. This meant our conversations and interviews could be much longer and more rambling.

Now, this goes against *everything* they tell you about creating and producing a podcast: keep it tight, keep it relevant and keep it as short as possible. By giving ourselves the freedom to talk for as long as we wanted and the space to explore more with our guests, we were breaking all the rules of podcasting and broadcasting. But it meant we were having free-ranging conversations with no set structure or agenda that were more akin to the real conversations you have in the pub. Our guests felt like they were sitting in a pub with us having a chat – and that meant our listeners felt they were sharing the table and enjoying it, too. It made the podcast more intimate and showed more of ourselves and our lives (which was troubling at the start, until people said they wanted more).

One thing we also did really badly was sound quality. We hadn't invested in any new equipment and were just recording off our laptops. But a funny thing happened: this became part of the charm of the podcast. It made us sound different. Anyone who was put off by the sound quality probably wasn't the ideal listener anyway. And it became a running joke (just look at the reviews on iTunes).

'LET THEM WEAR MERCH'

Our next major milestone was merchandise. I'd never envisaged myself in a situation where I'd become a T-shirt retailer, but we thought it would be good to rock up at a race or two in a BBR vest or T-shirt so we could get a picture and the community would love it. It was never the intention to start selling these to the wider community. I mean, who wears branded merchandise from a podcast? Seriously?

For our first running top, we decided to do something really simple: full red with a giant 'Bad Boy Running' logo on the front, with a quote from one of our podcasts on the back.

Since the launch of the Facebook group, we'd got to know which quotes people liked. On an episode about whether I should join a running club or not, David made the comment that 'the problem with running clubs is… they're full of runners', meaning that runners were usually quite introspective and may not come across as welcoming at first. But that quote resonated with the community and we decided to use it on the back of the top. We had a couple made… and when the photos of us wearing them in races came through, the call for us to sell them more widely was loud.

It works. It worked for us with the podcast and community. It worked for my own businesses and brands. It worked for the brands and businesses I've been involved with since. And it will work for you.

Doing the right things in the right way has led to opportunities and places we never expected. We've opened up the door to speak to some of the running world's biggest names, who were intrigued about coming on our little podcast simply because they'd been told by their running pals that it would be a fun experience. As a result, BBR was invited by the National Running Show in the UK to host an entire 'Ultra Zone' for the ultrarunning community at its Birmingham event. It was a little oversubscribed...

Something clicked. It was a genuine revelation that doing things differently from other podcasts was the basis of the 'secret sauce'

that made this work. The freedom to step into who we really were and how we really wanted to talk to our audience was the catalyst for the transformation. It was personality unleashed.

We polarised – and possibly alienated – some listeners, who were used to the more sedate pace (ironically) of other running podcasts and running media. But that was good. What is the point of hanging on to listeners and followers who want you to be something other than you are? By drawing a line in the sand and actively discouraging the wrong people from listening and joining the community, we strengthened and deepened our relationship with those who bought wholesale into our way of doing things.

So many brands, podcasts and communities reek of that terrible stench of desperation. They're all so eager to be friends with everybody and not offend, to stay on the right side of sponsors and the industry. Leaving all that behind was a huge part of our community's success.

We've since got sponsorship, sold a ton more merchandise and now have opportunities flowing to us rather than the other way around. And, quite improbably, David and I are now presidents of the Bad Boy Running Club, an England Athletics-affiliated running club where they actually do running and stuff. It goes without saying that England Athletics has never had a club inside the walls of its membership so critical and difficult to handle, and it's only a matter of time before we get chucked out. We wouldn't want it any other way.

Beyond that, our little cult still feels like a cult. It hasn't jumped the shark by doing anything to damage our relationship with our audience. We still record every Monday like clockwork and still talk absolute bollocks about anything and everything on episodes that often last three hours. And the sound quality is still really quite terrible. But that just doesn't matter.

A cult, though, is built on foundations that are more important than details. If you've read this and you're now thinking you can go set up a Facebook group, print a few T-shirts and encourage your audience to shout obscenities at each other and you'll have a ready-made cult, you will fail. The purpose of the story is to show you what is possible when you leave behind your constraints and step into the role of cult leader. There is a foundation upon which you need to build a cult, but there is an order and it requires you to be the leader you've probably always been a bit too scared to become. I don't mean to sound contrarian, but you're going to have to make some decisions if you want to go full cult on your audience. The rewards are there – are you prepared to make the step?

IF YOU KNOW THAT, BUT AREN'T DOING ANYTHING ABOUT IT, THEN...

Knowing what to do is only one part of the equation. Actually doing something about it is a whole different story.

If knowledge were the only impediment to people becoming anything they wanted, the world would be swarming with happy, fulfilled Renaissance millionaires. I hope I'm not spoiling anything for you by telling you that it is categorically not that way.

Everything you want and need to know is available to you at the click of a button thanks to the World Wide Web. (There's also a whole world of stuff you wish you didn't know and now can't unsee – but that's another story.)

What I'm saying is that 'knowing' and 'doing' are worlds apart.

If you're an avid reader of business books or, like me, a self-help junkie, you 'know' a ton of stuff that will grow your business, take you to 'the next level' or help you live a fulfilled and balanced life.

However, the fact that you're still arguing with your bookkeeper over petty expenses not being properly completed, that you regularly hit your head against the wall because your revenue growth has stalled, or that you're staring at this book blankly and lacking in all emotion after staying up till 3am binge-watching Netflix and eating Doritos shows us that knowledge doesn't always equal action.

If I were going all Tony Robbins on your ass, I'd start by proclaiming some grand formula about why we don't do things even when we know they will benefit us in the long term. It's all about pain versus pleasure. If the pain of doing something is more than the pain of doing nothing, we'll always stick with the lesser pain.

Anyone who has ever completed a self-assessment tax return will know exactly what I mean. The pain of collating your receipts, figuring out how much you've been paid, going back through endless statements and – ugh – even writing about it sends you into a self-induced coma of boredom. So you put it off and put it off, until finally, 29 January hits and you think 'maybe I should do something about it'. With your accountant cursing you (and every other one of their clients who thinks the same), your pain

"

There are no rational reasons for you staying stuck where you are right now

balance tips towards action rather than getting fined, and suddenly you kick into action. You can replace this example with writing essays, making sales calls, credit control... whatever action has associated pains.

But that's not all. We're emotional animals. We worry about things. That's only human. Even if we don't consciously understand how we act, we only act in line with how we feel. And our delicate little egos have some basic needs: we want to be loved, we want to feel comfortable and we want to be respected. Doesn't that sound nice? Ahhh!

There's just one problem: sometimes, our brains can be right dicks. They don't want us to do *anything* that causes us discomfort. They're like an overprotective mother who doesn't want you to try anything because she's worried your frail little body and mind can't cope with disappointment or shame or failure.

Some of the ideas in this book may have been said before, and you may have heard them articulated by others. But they have never been put together as they are in this book – as a winning formula that is proven to work– and especially not without all the sparkling wit and humour. And there's a story or two in here that have most definitely not been indexed by Google yet.

I'm not going to show you that cheesy graphic explaining how 'your future can be found beyond the edge of your comfort zone', or any motivational shizz like that. It's just worth noting that sometimes (and by this I mean most of the time), we act cautiously for reasons we often don't understand. They are emotional reasons that we try to justify rationally and logically. Don't be fooled, though. There are no rational reasons for you staying stuck where you are right now. Your emotions are your own business. The fact is that if you don't want to stay in the 20% where *nothing* happens even though you know you should do something, it's time to tackle this.

Look, at one stage I was like this too. I knew I needed to make big changes and I still didn't do anything about it. More than that— I continued to grow my business the conventional way. To do what everyone else did, but do more of it. Appeal to the same audiences everyone else did. Talk like everyone else did. It was a mediocre strategy that produced mediocre results. Not bad results, not exceptionally good results... just... well, 'meh' results. And that's the problem. You may not be feeling the pain of losing clients week after week or watching your sales dive as a hip new upstart competitor hoovers up your market share. It's often a more mundane and chronic drip-drip effect of feeling your energy and your hopes for a killer business seep away.

You see, 'meh' marketing is better than no marketing. It works— to an extent. However, it will never give you exceptional results. It won't help you stamp your mark on your industry or transform your company into a red-hot customer magnet. It certainly won't get you talked about, nor turn your existing customers into rabid fans frothing at the mouth for your products.

It comes down to a choice. If you want to be insanely good, you have to be a bit insane. I am. But I didn't used to be; I was very sensible once, and I was also almost broke. Deep down in me, I had this ever-present churning feeling that I should be bolder and braver with the way I was showing up. Heck, it's what I told the companies I worked with – so why wasn't I doing it myself?

A number of objections had entered my head and lodged themselves there far too firmly for far too long. These are the same powerful objections that will likely slow you down and hold you back from doing what needs to be done. And that's why we're going to take a baseball bat to some of them right now.

OBJECTION #1: 'EVERYTHING MIGHT COME CRUMBLING DOWN'

You're going to lead with this one? Total apocalypse as the opening gambit? OK. No worries.

There are three possible paths for your business, and one of those is total annihilation. Fire, brimstone, tears, a P45, a stampeding mob of angry creditors and a bonfire of hopes and dreams. You get the picture. This is the least likely outcome of taking any action. Only companies that totally fuck up are likely to collapse in this spectacular Enron style; unless you're dealing in sub-prime mortgages, Facebook user data or other highly unethical practices, sudden death just isn't likely to be on the cards. On the other hand, if you were going to go, what a way to go.

Sadly, life is rarely that exciting. What is more likely – and much, much worse – is a slow, painful death. At least if you crash and burn, it's quick and you can start to recover; a veritable clear-out to make way for the new. I'm not saying that's your path and you should pack up and start again, but if that were to be your choice, then it's clean, isn't it? Not so for most businesses.

It's time for a graph. Here's one showing typical company growth:

THE GROWTH/DECLINE CURVE

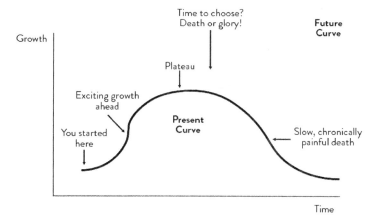

On here, you have a few years of strong upward growth until you plateau. Most people look at the growth bit, salivating about how to return to that state. But look again at what typically comes after the growth. It's not just a plateau – it's a slow, gradual decline. If you're in a business going through such a decline, it's not a pretty sight.

Granted, you don't have the sudden exodus of staff or sales revenue crises. You're not unexpectedly usurped by a young upstart or watching over the collapse of your customer/client base. No –

it happens gradually, almost imperceptibly. Like a frog boiled in a pot. Or a lobster. Or any other aquatic creature that needs to fix that pretty important evolutionary trait.

If you do nothing, the odds tell us this will be your path. This is what happens to the majority of businesses that sit on their hands and try to carry on as normal. By the time the founder or leaders finally wake up to the long drawn-out decline, it's often too late.

So, no; by being bold and brave and deciding to take action on this, you're not risking everything collapsing around you. In fact, you're protecting yourself against an even worse fate: slow decline.

You've already succeeded where so many businesses have failed by growing your business to the size it is and surviving this long. But now it's time to shift gears on an approach that will restart the momentum you had at the beginning, rekindle the energy in your team and customers, and bring the excitement back to growing your brand.

The next objection is almost the reverse of #1.

OBJECTION #2: 'I'D LOSE WHAT I BUILT UP. CUSTOMERS COULD ABANDON ME'

Those first few years in business running my agency were all hustle and grind. Winning every one of my clients seemed like an uphill battle that took ages. After a couple of years standing at the top of the hill looking down, it felt like I'd worked damned hard to get where I was. Then that sinking feeling hit – I needed to protect what I had. I'd worked so hard to get there that no way was I going to do anything that threatened what I had.

So I ring-fenced and turned from offence to defence. Big mistake. I abandoned the way I did things to 'get serious' in my agency.

I went from crazy fun (subjective) advertising promotions that saw me mailing all kinds of weird things to prospective clients – voodoo dolls, Valentine's cards, fake money – and shooting scrappy, handheld videos that my audience used to love, to wearing shirts, changing the website to look 'more professional' and having business cards and compliment slips printed. (I mean, seriously. Why the fuck did we ever sacrifice good trees for compliment slips?) I turned my back on my old ways because I was worried that now I had built my business to a certain size, it was time to consolidate and go after bigger clients.

There's a great saying that has been bastardised and misattributed in so many ways, but was originally coined by Marshall Goldsmith: 'What got you here, won't get you there.' This makes a really good point about needing to constantly upgrade your thinking. It is hugely misinterpreted, though, and many feel like it means you need to change. You don't. In fact, by not adhering to the same values that drove your business or brand in the first place, you almost sacrifice the energy and momentum that got you to where you are. Ask yourself, how different does your business look and feel from the days back when you experienced crazy fast growth and it felt like you were on top of the world? I'll bet it's pretty different.

Rather than losing what you built up and watching customers abandon you, you need to reconnect with why you did this in the first place. The reason brands run out of steam and struggle is because they lose that connection. I'm here, right now, to remind you that this approach is simply a return to how it used to be. Sure, the execution may be a bit different, but it worked. In this book I'm going to show you how to achieve it.

Before we continue, I need to be honest with you. When you strike out with a bold new approach, you will probably lose some customers. Whenever it feels like a business or brand is shifting up a gear, there are going to be customers or clients who worry about change and worry about how that change will affect them. And this is going to hurt – they don't care about your growth. They care about how you serve them and what you do for them. And often, it makes them uncomfortable to see you changing and growing. Like when you come back to your little hometown after university to find that your friends who never moved away just aren't in the same place as you any more. You grow apart.

Like a soap storyline about an extramarital affair or an alienated lover, let me put my arm around you and confidently tell you this: 'You don't need them. You're better than that. And there are plenty more fish in the sea.' All of those are true. And those fish are going to end up being your biggest goddamn cheerleaders. For now, drain away all concerns about customers abandoning you and let's worry about your oh-so-precious reputation.

OBJECTION #3: 'I'D GET NEGATIVE PUSHBACK AND MY REPUTATION COULD BE MUD'

It's always useful to understand the motivation behind any criticism or objections you receive about the direction of your business. Individuals who have seemingly never given two hoots about the growth of my business or its future will suddenly pop up to deliver advice about what I should be doing, what I shouldn't be doing, and how to conduct myself. And it's not just on the outside; people within your own team may suddenly become concerned about how you come across or what your actions may do for your business.

We're human and as such, we do one thing really, really well: think about ourselves all the time. Although we may not be doing it consciously, we're in self-protection mode most of the time. We don't like feeling threatened or worthless or worried about things that may upset our delicate state of affairs. So we criticise and gossip and do all those chimp-brain-friendly activities we think will help.

Criticism and negativity are just two of those things. When you receive unsolicited criticism, understand that it's never about you – it's all about the individual giving the criticism. In some way, you have threatened or challenged a state of affairs they have become comfortable with, and this is their way of coping. Don't blame them. They may not even realise they're doing it; they just think they're being helpful and honest with you, pointing out the 'truth'. In fact, they're pushing back on something that doesn't benefit them.

It's why other agency owners tell me that my approach isn't right for getting clients, or offer me advice I never asked for on how to run my agency. They don't like what I do – partly because it threatens them, and partly because if it's successful it may force them to change what they're doing to keep up. And no one likes change.

But for some reason, we put greater weight on the opinions of our peers and colleagues than we should. Ask yourself: if someone goes out of their way to give you negative feedback, what's in it for them? Maybe they're not cut out for big, bold change. Maybe *you're* not, and they have a point.

Certainly, you should seek out feedback and objective help to improve your business and brand. That is not in doubt. When you start your cult-building process and every other business around you suddenly sits up and takes notice of the fact you're causing ripples in your industry or sector, just listen to the negative pushback come in.

And on that point…

OBJECTION #4: 'I'LL BE JUDGED'

If there's one thing I can guarantee, it's this: you *will* be judged.

And that's exactly what you want to happen. Because when you're being judged, it means you're being noticed – and *nearly* all publicity is good publicity.

When we launched our cult podcast, we were almost insiders forced onto the outside. We had little to lose, so being judged didn't affect us. We simply didn't care what those in our industry thought of us – and it showed in the abandon with which we talked about anything and everything we could.

When you have nothing to lose, this is easy. It's harder when you feel there is a lot at stake. But it goes back to the point above that those judging you often have motivations beyond anything you can or ever will influence.

You have to get used to this one point. You have to get used to being judged. You don't have to like it or enjoy it, although at a certain point it does become a benchmark of how well you're doing, as I'll explain later.

The first time you get a hater is a defining moment. There's nothing you can do about it. Some stranger on the internet has decided they don't like you and has no problem whatsoever telling you to your face. At this point you make a choice:

1. You decide to worry about it, confront the hater and see if you can come to a point of accommodation, or

2. You say 'fuck it' and move on.

Believe me, I've tried both approaches and I can categorically tell you that the first one doesn't work; the second one is the best way to deal with most expressions of judgement.

This doesn't mean turning a blind eye if someone is rude, offensive, racist, sexist, anything else-ist, or libellous. Go after that mofo. But, for the most part, having a healthy dose of 'who cares?' goes a long way to keeping you focused on the prize.

Let them judge all they want when you're resting your head on a bed of money in a few years' time.

OBJECTION #5: 'THE CHANGE IS GOING TO BE HARD WORK/A HASSLE'

Yes, it is.

But not nearly as much hard work and hassle as presiding over a brand or business that needs to arrest its slow decline and has lost all relevance to its customers and market.

Time to put on those big boy/girl pants and deal with it.

OBJECTION #6: 'IF THIS DOESN'T WORK, I'M GOING TO LOOK LIKE AN IDIOT'

If I had the choice between looking like an idiot and feeling like an idiot, I'd definitely want to avoid the latter.

This isn't just an approach to marketing and attracting and keeping customers. Becoming a cult leader transforms your business.

You can picture how well it will go down with your senior team now. You call a meeting to discuss 'forward strategy' (you should never call a meeting with that title, by the way). They're sitting nervously around the table in anticipation of your arrival. Hushed whispers only guess at what you want to announce. As you walk through the door, all eyes turn eagerly to you, everyone poised to hear what nugget of wisdom you're planning to drop.

What they don't expect you to say is…

'We're going to start a cult.'

If you can picture that, you can also picture the looks of confusion and the glazed eyes trying to hide their owners' thoughts of spending the next few hours tidying up their CV in readiness for a job search.

It's a big, bold, brave move, and one your team don't expect. But hell – if your team don't expect it, it's going to totally blindside your competitors.

One of the reasons is that people don't ever want to join a cult. They join something that interests them. You *end up* in a cult; you don't purposefully join one. And you'd be insane if you did.

But once you're in, you're in. Separate the features of being in a cult for your team:

- Gaining a renewed and singular focus

- Living our values

- Having a cohesive purpose

- Deepening our relationship with customers (perhaps fewer customers/clients).

Rephrase the benefits of being in a cult, and it sounds like a veritable checklist of the best parts of a great company culture! That's because a great culture attracts and retains new talent.

If you choose to do it and it doesn't pan out, you may look like an idiot. If you choose not to do it at all, you'll avoid looking like an idiot, certainly. But you'll feel like an even bigger idiot for not giving it a shot.

OBJECTION #7: 'THIS IS A GOOD IDEA, BUT NOT NOW. NOW IS NOT THE RIGHT TIME'

If something is a good idea, it's a good idea *right now*. Why delay doing something you know is the future of your business, that you know can jump-start momentum and get your team firing on all cylinders again? Because of fear.

As Yoda once said in an aberration of a prequel I'll not name: 'Fear is the path to the Dark Side. Fear leads to anger. Anger leads to hate. Hate leads to suffering.' Well, you can skip the anger bit and make fear go straight to suffering – because not taking action on something that has the power to make a difference to you and your brand will lead to your suffering. You're probably suffering right now. If you're anxious that your competition is gnawing away at your market share, if you're worried about keeping your team around you and together, if you're concerned that everything you built up is at risk of falling apart because you can't pull your message together in a way that allows you to strike decisively in your market, suffering is the start of how you feel. (Hopefully you won't turn to the Dark Side, though.)

The truth is, it's never the right time and it's also always the right time. How's that for a cryptic piece of advice?

You've been in business long enough to know there is always a crisis, there is always pressure on your team's time and capacity, and you're always up against it, back against the wall and fighting to stay on top of everything. That will always be the case. But time is running out. The silent drip, drip, drip of your business's energy leaking away until it's barely alive means you need to act now. And that's why 'right now' is also the right time.

READY? LET'S GO

We've aired all the objections that typically kill action dead and have dealt with each one in turn. Now is the time to take a bold step.

When you do exactly what I'm going to show you in this book, you start to transform how you work. The process of attracting and keeping customers becomes easier. You choose who you want to have in your world and you actively repel those, to put it lightly, absolute fucking nightmare clients and customers. Someone else can deal with them. You move from being price sensitive to not having to worry about pricing in quite the same way. This system shows how you never need lurch from crisis to crisis because you build something so strong within your brand and your messaging that it acts as a more powerful force than any transient customer retention scheme or brand loyalty initiative. (I almost threw up in my mouth writing those words.)

When you step up and step into the role of cult leader, everything changes. It doesn't necessarily require huge root-and-branch change from the outset. A few simple, bold changes are all it takes to start this journey and put your business or brand back on the track to being relentless again. But you do need to take the first step.

YOUR RECIPE FOR A CULT

Before we go on, there's an important issue we need to address. Sure, starting and growing your own band of devoted cult members sounds just swell and dandy, but are you primed to be able to do it in the first place?

You don't just get to start a cult without getting all your ducks in a row. Yep, I'm talking about goddamn criteria. (I warned you this wasn't a book for everyone.)

RULE #1: YOU NEED A GOOD PRODUCT OR SERVICE

If you've got a great product or service to start with, you're off to a flier. But if your product or service sucks the big one, this is not going to work for you. Your audience aren't idiots. This process is deep. If you bring a turkey to this shoot, you're going to get found out pretty quickly and you'll struggle to make it work.

This isn't really about having a good product or service, though; that should be a given if you're going to start and grow a cult. More than anything, what you need to demonstrate is a commitment to your followers.

RULE #2: YOU NEED TO COMMIT TO YOUR FOLLOWERS

There's no shortcut here. If you're not committed to your audience, this is going to be a painful, tortuous journey.

If you're the kind of douchebag who wants a band of zombies to buy from you at your command, then: a) you're going to be very disappointed, and b) fuck you. You're not a leader, you're an asshole. Seriously, spare yourself the time and effort and give up now.

I don't believe that's you. My approach requires you to step into being the leader you always wanted to be. That means keeping in mind the interests, desires and worries of your cult followers. It means getting under their skin to understand how they feel, and speaking to them on a deep emotional level. That's what great leaders do.

When you're really tuned in to your audience, that's when the magic happens. Yes, they're following you, but the really powerful moves start when you listen to them. You can give them exactly what they want, even if they can't articulate it.

You're no longer 'selling' to them; your devotees are buying from you. They buy from you because every time they buy, it adds greater strength to their desire to belong and identify as a member of the cult. There's no such thing as objections and resistance when your brand becomes part of your followers' identity.

RULE #3: YOU NEED TO COMMIT TO THIS PROCESS

I know from experience working with leaders and their teams that there may be times when you're hit by self-doubt and fearful of whether this will work. When you go big, that's what happens. It feels scary because it *is*. One of the best quotes I heard from a lady who rowed across the Atlantic several times was this: 'The thing about getting out of your comfort zone is that it feels uncomfortable.' She's right. If you're doing this and you don't feel uncomfortable, you're probably doing it wrong. Push on, lean in, do whatever it takes to get through the weirdness, and it will start to make sense.

And don't worry – I'll be by your side all the way. Whether that's giving you more examples or providing support through the Facebook group, we'll get your cult launched and growing.

RULE #4: YOU NEED TO KEEP AN OPEN MIND

Another prerequisite for making this work is an open mind. What I'll show you in the next few chapters is going to be surprising and counterintuitive, and will probably challenge your

66

*Being bold means
zagging when others
are zigging*

99

ideas about how to grow a following. You're not going to find flimsy, vague suggestions, like 'grow your social media following' or 'engage with your followers'. They may work for someone else's method, but not this one. That's why it's imperative that you keep an open mind, do the exercises and commit to the process.

RULE #5: YOU NEED TO BE BOLD

Everything you're about to learn is primarily focused on one thing: to accentuate the bold and be different. If you've zero intention of stepping up to the plate, save yourself a few hours and leave the book here. A quote often attributed to Henry Ford states: 'If you keep doing the same thing, you'll always get the same results.'

It's crazy how many leaders and brands spout this phrase whenever they get the chance. Yet their actions show anything but divergence from what everyone else is doing.

Being bold means zagging when others are zigging, communicating and connecting in ways other brands don't. By definition, it means being different and stepping outside what you may be used to doing.

Ask yourself: did your previous approach work? Have any of the strategies you've used to grow your business worked for you? If the answer is no – and I imagine it is, if you're reading this book – then bold is the path to take.

Bold also means no half-measures. Don't be half-arsed and non-committal when you dive into the exercises. Say what you really feel. Act how you really want to act. Yes, it may scare you, but I guarantee it will feel liberating and – dare I say it – inspiring.

Remember, being bold doesn't mean stumbling around like a corporate Larry David being a dick to whoever crosses your path. Being bold means standing for something and not being afraid to stand up whenever and wherever you are to communicate, defend and promote that message.

Acting bold and being fearless is about confidence. You get confidence when you see results. It's like a muscle – the more you flex it, the stronger you become. It becomes a habit and you step into boldness and confidence all the time. Being bold becomes what you do because it comes from a natural and authentic place.

Ugh – the A-word again. I hate it when self-help gurus vomit about being your 'authentic self' without giving you any idea of what that hopeless phrase actually means. What will help you, though, is this:

RULE #6: YOU NEED STRONG VALUES

When you started out with your vision of your brand, you knew what you wanted to do and what you didn't want to do. You may not have created a set of values in that wanky Silicon-Valley-office sort of way that branding pros like me get paid the big bucks to help you with (and it is totally worth doing, by the way). But you probably had a really clear idea about what you *didn't* want to be.

You probably knew which businesses or brands you didn't want to end up like. There are so many examples of how not to do things. And they're there to help you get it right.

I'm going to need you to time travel right now and go back to how you felt when you started your business. What did you want to achieve? What did you hope your business was going to turn out like?

If you've watched any time travel movies, you'll know all about screwy timelines and how big decisions can change the course of your trajectory. What they don't tell you is that lots of small decisions can knock you off course, as well; a compromise here, a shrinking back there, a decision delayed because you were unsure – all these add up to pushing you in a direction that isn't what you imagined when you started.

What is the gap between where you are now and where you believe you should be? If it feels huge, then as *The Hitchhiker's Guide to the Galaxy* says, 'don't panic!' What I show you in this book will help you reconnect with your values and what you wanted your business or brand to become.

THE CULT COMMANDMENTS

❝

In Tyler we trusted.

FIGHT CLUB

The first rule of Cult Club is: you don't talk about Cult Club.

Only kidding – I want you to talk about starting and building your cult as much as you can. (These books aren't going to sell themselves, y'know.)

In the previous chapters, we've kicked to the kerb any notion that brand loyalty and the traditional way of marketing and promoting your brand still work, if they ever worked at all. We've discovered why starting and growing a cult is the best possible vehicle for developing a stronger, more powerful connection with your audience and fostering belonging.

We've also looked at how the process of building a cult isn't for everyone. Building a cult is a bold move. It requires bravery and the ability to take your team, company and community with you when you go for it. When you need help, I'm here for you (just visit **www.cultbrandmethod.com** or get more support at **www. facebook.com/groups/howtostartacult**).

It may be lonely up there, but there's a good reason. The spoils of this particular battle for the minds of your audience will go to those who are prepared to stand up, stand out and step into becoming a cult leader who commits.

BE BOLD, BREAK RULES… JUST DON'T BREAK *THESE* RULES

Putting a torch to the rulebook is something I'll encourage you to do as much as possible in the execution of this plan. But there are seven rules – let's call them 'commandments'– that you absolutely, positively must follow to make this a success.

This isn't optional. Do one without the others, and it won't work. Do six without one, and it won't work. I'm being strict for a reason. We need to get through this.

To explain why I take this approach, let's talk diets. (No, I'm not saying you need one. You look great.) Diets tell us everything about human behaviour.

Why is it easier to follow an Atkins diet or any mega-strict diet that cuts out entire food groups (no sugar, no carbs, no alcohol) or focuses on eating one food type (the grapefruit diet, the cabbage soup diet) than simply to eat more healthily?

When you're told to eat better or consume fewer calories, the instruction is just too vague. There are too many variables and combinations of what you *could* do. This lack of clarity makes it easy to give up.

When you have a more binary choice, it's simple to put into action. Eat this; don't eat that. It's black and white.

So think of these commandments as your diet. Stick with this to get the results you want. Any deviation and it won't work. I don't apologise for going all authoritarian – we're running a serious operation to get you where you need to be as quickly and painlessly as possible.

Interestingly, this brings into play one of the key features of a cult, which is the balance between the individual and the group. When we're laying down the law, group members are expected to fall into line with the needs of the wider group to gain the benefits of belonging, identity and being part of something bigger than themselves.

Build a strong enough message and deliver it in the right way, and your followers will be prepared to be part of your cult

There's a wider point to be understood by the importance of these commandments, and that is: you should not be afraid to set rules yourself. Build a strong enough message and deliver it in the right way, and your followers will be prepared to be part of your cult.

Another function of these commandments is to focus on action. Without sounding like a hippie when I talk about energy, there is a great truth in the belief that energy creates more energy. As we discovered with the BBR cult, continued and persistent action was the best way to cultivate the cult following, get the members engaged with each other and build momentum and virality around the brand. Which is a really roundabout way of saying: just keep doing stuff and don't stand still. Neglect this for any amount of time in the early days and you may struggle to get the momentum going again.

Presenting these commandments in this way has another more practical purpose. Commandments are made to be read, digested and acted upon. There's a reason God slapped them onto a couple of slabs of rock for Moses to bring down the mountain: he intended Moses to share his commandments with the gathered crowd.

I'm not saying you're Moses or that you need to spread the word with quite the same vigour, but those in your team who are going to be responsible for undertaking this and building a cult from the ground up need to know the commandments. They need to know exactly what steps to take to get from where they are now to where you plan the brand to be.

These commandments should be treated as such. More importantly, they should provide a guide for you as the leader taking your team and audience through this process. Tear this page out, place the commandments where you can see them every day, and use them as your handbook to refer to whenever you feel your message is being lost or diluted. Use these commandments. Follow them to the letter. Do not deviate from your path.

You need to commit to the commandments– or decide right now that you don't have what it takes and that maybe another approach might work. There's no need to be ashamed about being realistic and knowing in yourself that this may be a little too much for you. If we're being honest, it feels... well, a bit... cult-y, unsurprisingly. Embrace that feeling of weirdness, because if you're going to find it hard to cope with now, the rest of this journey is going to be a struggle.

So, here it is.

This is your last chance to escape and turn your back on what is going to be a fun but undoubtedly bizarre ride.

But the honest truth is that you probably won't action any of the commandments I've laid out below, nor share them with your team or start working towards them. And that's fine. Only a few readers will read these commandments, take them as gospel and get to work. (Even if you're reading this with zero chance of implementing this or getting all the benefits, you'll still get something from this book you can take away.)

THE CULTBRAND MODEL

So, here we are. Like Dorothy about to set off on her journey on the yellow brick road after callously murdering an old lady, you're probably trepidatious and not a little uncertain about what this is going to entail. To that I say...

I've got you. No excuses or turning back now. We're in this together.

I'm about to introduce you to the seven Cult Commandments that will give you the framework you need as a future cult leader to start and grow your cult. Yes, there may be other ways of doing it, but these commandments come from my own experience building cults and working with clients to establish cult-like devotion from their followers. I've worked with businesses across the spectrum, from high-flying technology brands that want to make their apps stickier and their followers more devoted, to legal services firms that break the mould of what you'd expect from blood-sucking, extortionate-hourly-fee-charging lawyers. I've seen this work for coaches, training platforms, service businesses – in fact, any business that attracts an audience. Many thought they needed thousands of followers, but they realised that even a small but devoted following was enough to seriously kick-start their business.

There are seven steps within the CultBrand model. Having seen the way the BBR cult developed, I took the best parts from the cult-building process and combined it with systems I used to grow businesses and brands. Without realising it, we'd applied all the tried and tested methods used by marketers and brand experts to get the message out there, differentiate ourselves from the competition and stand out. Building a CultBrand amplified its impact. I realised that if I could get leaders to shift into this bolder way of thinking and stop being afraid of saying 'no' to anyone and everyone that they, too, could build a cult following.

You can't, of course, start from scratch. You've already got a business or brand and you need to keep turning the wheels while you start the process of transformation.

There is an important mindset shift that needs to accompany this process. You have to both care and not care. If someone wants to be your pal, that's great. But it needs to be on *your* terms. Too many business owners feel they have to shape-shift to appeal to a broader audience or contort what they do to keep their customers on side.

No one likes a chameleon, so you still need to stick to your principles. But you have to hold a healthy neutrality about your following. You will lose some who have been with you; not everyone likes change. Let go of them.

Don't waste your attention, care and energy on those who don't join your cult. You're going to need all that energy for the devotees who do.

And that's where you're differentiating yourself from most brands. They put a ton of focus on gaining new followers, friends and customers. It's the damn wrong way round. Their focus should be on the people who are already followers, friends and customers, and deepening that relationship. Shift the focus, and it flips the switch on your brand having organic magnetism, effortlessly attracting the right people under your banner thanks to your energy, momentum and the pulling power of your followers.

That's why following the seven Cult Commandments is essential and why you should do so unquestioningly, like every good cult follower. This model was designed to be followed in order, and every part is critical to your end mission to start and grow a cult.

What I will show you has been carefully engineered based on my experience and having worked with hundreds of businesses, from small one-person consultancies looking to grow to large fintech brands with global ambitions. It works for businesses of every size. It works across every industry. You can do this yourself or work with a qualified CultBrand coach to bring this to life for your business and start your cult.

GET INVOLVED

Sign up to the 'How to Start a Cult' mini-course for more help. Register for free here: **www.cultbrandmethod.com**

THE ULTIMATE PRIZE

Like any good recovery programme, it's all about the steps. But instead of recovering from a drug addiction, this programme is going to help you recover from mediocrity, inertia and lack of momentum.

When you follow this model in the right order and with the right level of application, you will see major changes in how you lead, how your brand is perceived and how you build your relationship with your followers, fans and customers.

The CultBrand process will help you:

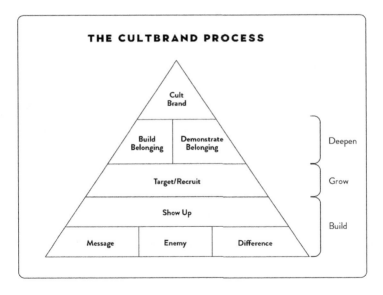

HOW TO GET YOUR TEAM ON BOARD

The first set of followers you have to win over are those closest to you. No, not your cat (she'll never follow you or anyone – she's a cat), but your team.

If even they don't buy into your dream of a cult, the chances that you'll ever get to full cult-like status are slim.

Your team is almost like your own gang of cult leaders or lieutenants. They need to be sold on the idea before anyone else. Get that right and everything will fall into place.

Here are some of the ways to get your team on board.

Connect with your vision

You have (or at least had) a big vision of what you wanted your business to be. How long has it been since you brought your team together to reconnect with that vision – or even discuss whether it still *is* the vision? When you get back to thinking about what you want from the business and where you want it to be, you open up the discussion about how to get there – and whether what you're doing is working or not. Importantly with these discussions, allow others to connect what they want with the vision. If they see how their hopes, dreams and aspirations are more likely to be fulfilled by going down the cult-building track, they'll jump on board.

Go back to fundamentals

Sometimes you need to take a step back before going forward. To sell your team on the idea of building a cult following, they need to genuinely believe there is a distinct need for it. If they don't feel there is any danger in pursuing the current path or sticking to what you've always done, they'll never buy in. A good way is to do an open audit of where you are now. If some team members think everything is hunky-dory, they won't be receptive. If they're clear on the challenge ahead, you have a better chance of persuading them a different tack is needed. Bring your team together and workshop about your current situation and what the gap is between where you are now and where you want to be. Be clear, honest and open, and encourage your team to do the same.

Get the most enthusiastic on board first

You may have one member of the team who has a bit more pizzazz than the others. They're the one who is always ready to jump in first and get things going when others are more cautious. You're going to need that person right now. Win them over with your vision of what you can do.

Allow your team to own the idea

Give your team the creative freedom to make it work and put it into action. It may be your idea to start building a cult following, but within those parameters there's a huge amount of room for your team's ideas and creativity. How your cult looks and acts should be shaped by your discussions.

Show rather than tell

One of the ways that we successfully win clients as an agency is by showing them how funny and creative their cult could look when they've taken action. All too often we're used to seeing what other brands are doing and wishing we'd thought of it first or were doing something similarly creative.

Use the same idea to sell the concept of building a cult to your team, but start with curiosity rather than diktat. One good approach that works well is finding and showing examples of what other brands are doing and asking the following questions of your team:

- How do we do the same?

- How could we make this work for our business/brand?

- What would it take to make this happen here?

This usually provides a platform for discussion that opens minds and broadens thinking – enough to win them over to the ways of the cult.

INTRODUCING THE CULT COMMANDMENTS

OK, I'll stop being a tease now and reveal a little bit of leg to give you a cheeky overview of what the seven steps are and how they work together to build and grow your cult. I have rendered them in Old English, primarily to give them more gravitas, as befitting of a modern-day Moses.

1. Thou shalt develop a polarising cult message

Choose your central message and know how it differentiates you from everyone else vying for your audience's attention, putting clear space between you and them.

2. Thou shalt pick an enemy

Identify the source of your followers' woes, show them you're on their side and join them in throwing rocks. Metaphorically, of course.

3. Thou shalt be different. And celebrate it

Take the straight line to standing out and creating contrast against others in a visceral way that stirs your followers' emotions and hacks their brains.

4. Thou shalt bang thy drum over and over and over

Consistently show up for your cult devotees to deliver all the benefits quicker than you hoped possible – when you do it right.

5. Thou shalt target outliers and misfits

Understand who you are best placed to serve, and be the home for those who have none. Show them that you 'get' them.

6. Thou shalt build belonging

Deepen the relationship with your cult following so they feel compelled to go out, bang the drum for your brand and recruit other followers for you.

7. Thou shalt give thy followers plentiful opportunities to demonstrate belonging

Allow your followers to demonstrate their devotion in as many ways as possible so they can broadcast their belonging to each other and the wider world.

Brought together, these seven steps will make your competition irrelevant, kick-start sales and make your brand magnetic to the right kind of people who love what you do. This process will help you break through plateaus, secure the future of your brand and make life a whole lot more fun and fulfilling.

If you don't do the work, it is 100% guaranteed that you won't get the results and you will remain in the same position you are right now.

Do the work. Get the results. Ignore the voice in your head telling you you're mad (that voice may actually be your partner). And keep the faith. You can do this. So do it.

PART 2

HOW TO
START A CULT

THE MISSION

There are two distinct phases in the building and growth of a cult. The choices you make right at the start of this process and the decisions you arrive at, either based on your own insights or collectively as a team, will dictate how quickly you grow your cult and how effectively you can start attracting and indoctrinating new devotees to your cause.

This is a big step. This is the phase where you step into the role you never thought you'd hear yourself wishing to have. This marks the moment when you become a cult leader for the first time; when you move from zero to having your first cult member.

Sounds exciting, doesn't it? But you'd be well advised to avoid rushing headlong through this phase. The aim is not to simply get through this section and start the second phase.

As mentioned in Chapter 5, for the seven-step model to work, it needs to be completed in the correct order. This is a cult, for

Chrissake. There's no flexibility with a cult. Skipping ahead to deepening the relationship with your cult devotees will be more of a struggle if you choose not to work through the process exactly as I've laid it out in this book. And you can forget about flogging T-shirts to followers who aren't properly indoctrinated.

I know you may be impatient to get followers hooked on your brand in a way that has them falling at your knees to show their devotion to you... but hold your horses for a moment and dedicate the time you need to get this right first time.

THOU SHALT DEVELOP A POLARISING CULT MESSAGE

This is The Way.

THE MANDALORIAN

In this chapter, I show you:

- Why your lack of message is killing your momentum

- What every business gets wrong about its message

"

*The cult message
produces a
binary reaction*

"

- The one question your message needs to answer in the mind of your followers

- How to craft a message that draws the right followers to your cult.

Every cult needs a leader. Every cult leader needs a message. Like Mando, your cult's message needs to give your followers a clear and unequivocal direction: This is The Way. It's up to you to decide what The Way is for your cult.

A great cult message draws a line in the sand that has to be crossed by your cult devotees if they are to further strengthen their relationship with you. It is a statement or set of beliefs which they either agree with and believe in or disagree with and reject.

The cult message produces a binary reaction. It has to inspire agreement and acceptance from the follower, or disagreement and rejection. And it must take a clear and decisive position.

Mando trudges through the *Star Wars* universe trying to fend off the attacks on little Grogu, all the while keeping his armour on and following the strict creed of Mandalore. The cult message guides his actions and is central to his decision-making. The Way shows him the way.

The movie *Wall Street* garnered an almost religious following after Gordon Gekko's assertion that 'greed is good'. That was a clear position, and you either agree strongly or disagree strongly. So strong was this message that it led to an influx of young men wanting to become traders; such was the idolisation of Michael Douglas and the attitude in the roaring 80s. As an a-hole pin-stripe-suited trader, you were clear exactly what Gordon Gekko would do in any situation you found yourself in. That's a good, strong cult message.

Or look at the classic book, *Animal Farm* – a perfect example of using propaganda to achieve your nefarious aims. The mantra that all the animals are directed to follow– 'Four legs good, two legs bad'– sets the tone for everything that comes next. If you followed Napoleon and his Stalinist porcine leadership, you knew exactly who the enemy was and what the outlook for the cult was.

Each of these messages successfully polarises, provides clarity, provokes a positive or negative reaction (importantly, not just a neutral one) and serves as a guiding principle about how to act. We'll cover more as we move through this chapter, and we'll return to this point in other chapters.

WHY IS THE MESSAGE IMPORTANT?

The message attracts the attention of your very first follower. The message is the means by which your followers can go forth and attract more followers. A powerful message is key to unlocking momentum and growth.

Without a solid message, growing your following is hard; without it you can't hope to win new followers to your cause, tap into viral, organic growth, or build momentum.

If you struggle to gain traction or the attention you deserve, the message is the problem. If you struggle to cut through in your market while other brands always seem to get attention, the message is the problem. If you're constantly overlooked for media coverage and recognition, the message is the problem.

You can have the best product in the world, offer the best service and have a ton of cash to throw at marketing, but that doesn't mean a thing if you can't gain the attention of your target audience and make them sit up and take notice.

Brands that try to build a following often neglect this. They rush to promote their brand without realising that failing to nail their message will cost them. Big mistake.

Fail to get this right and everything is harder. Recruiting new followers is more difficult. It limits how quickly your following will grow organically. And you waste time, effort and money trying to drag people to your cause which could be used to accelerate your path to cult status.

With the right message, it won't feel like you're swimming against the tide. You don't need to throw time, money and effort at battling to win every follower to your cause.

A great message aligns with your ideal cult followers, and tells the wrong ones to fuck off. That way, you only end up with a cult base of those who truly love you – and it's love we want. Lots of it. (But not in an icky way; in a devoted, looking-at-you-like-you're-Jesus way.)

This isn't a cheeky optional extra to politely ponder over tea and biscuits. Oh no. You determine whether your cult lives or dies right now by how well you step up and get your message right. Polarisation is really important to determine whether people are aligned with you or not.

In other words: no message, no cult.

WHY NOW?

'But I don't need a message…'

'Do I really need a message?'

'What's wrong with what we're doing now?'

In the beginning, when you were growing your business or brand, you didn't need a message. Things were good, energy was high, sales were flooding in. So why do you need a message now?

I share your scepticism, and I understand this may feel like a huge step back. I mean, surely you know what your message is by now if you've grown your business to this point?

The purpose of your cult's message is to place you head and shoulders above your competitors. Achieving this is only possible for businesses that are prepared to walk a path no one else follows.

Other brands only have one message they're willing to broadcast. It's always about their product or service. That's it.

And here's the thing – it works. I'm not going to lie or try to trick you into thinking there is only one way. If you're persistent enough, are patient and have unlimited resources banging the product drum, then by sheer force of will, it can drive growth.

But it won't build you a cult following. It won't give you the tools to deepen your relationship with your audience so they recruit others to your brand. The old way is no longer the simplest, most straightforward path to where you want to go.

The mistake is believing that your message has to be about your product. In this chapter, I show you why you need to make an important shift to get this right.

Only by creating a powerful message do you create the conditions to build a cult following and an army of devotees ready to go into battle for you. When you take the right steps to get your message spot-on and know exactly what you want to broadcast to the world, everything falls into place.

THE LIGHTNING ROD

How do your devotees spread the word when they're unclear on the message? They don't, and that's why it's your job as cult leader to give them confidence. A clear, confident message breeds a clear, confident dissemination of your message.

The charismatic cult leader is the original messenger. Once the message is passed to the first, second and third follower, that message needs to spread. And spread like wildfire. It's not enough for a follower to simply 'like' you or 'follow' you. They need to be knee-deep in your message and cling to the belief that it is the right message for them.

An effective, powerful message has several characteristics. We'll deal with those below.

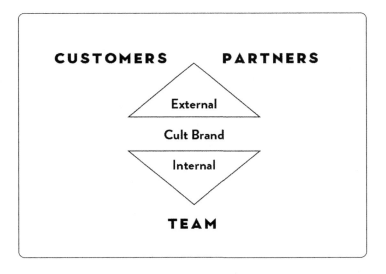

The message is the most important. As mentioned before, nothing happens until you get your first follower. And you'll never get your first follower until you communicate your message.

WHY EVERYTHING YOU (THINK YOU) KNOW ABOUT MESSAGING IS WRONG

EXERCISE

YOUR STARTING POINT

OK, it's not just going to be me talking here. It's time for you to chip in with your ideas.

So here's the first exercise of the book. Let's kick off by defining where you're starting from. The first step is to know where you are and what your message is; only then can you work on crafting a message that improves on it.

In this exercise, all I want you to do is write down below or on a piece of paper what your message is – or what you think your message is.

Don't rush this exercise. Take time to consider your answer.

You may have a clear message that you're actively using in your business. If so, this exercise will be over in seconds. If you don't have a specific message you're using, think about the kind of message you may be broadcasting to the world. Remember, regardless of whether you like it or not, you are sending out a message. You're either in control of it or you're not. Put another way: are you sending out good or bad vibes, man?

Good or bad, unhappy about it or defiantly proud of it – write it down.

....

....

....

....

....

....

....

....

....

....

....

Done it? Then let's analyse it and see how it stands up. To do this, it's more helpful to look at what a great message is *not* before we look at what makes a message great.

There are some common misconceptions and mistakes that brands make. Let's scotch those right now.

> **GET INVOLVED**
>
> Need help with digging up your message? Sign up to the 'How to Start a Cult' mini-course for more help. Register for free here: **www.cultbrandmethod.com**

What a message isn't

What your message should and shouldn't look like isn't hard to define. However, the water has been muddied.

The messages about your message are confusing. Marketing and brand experts deal out marketing concepts like cards at a poker table. Rather than clarify, they confuse. It's almost as though brand marketers don't want you to know how to do this yourself (hmm…).

It's not a sales pitch

A message is more than just 'BUY THIS! BUY THIS NOW!' But you could decide to present your message this way. It's no exaggeration to say that 99% of businesses and brands choose this as their primary message.

There's only one problem: this message only appeals to people who are ready to buy exactly what you are offering *right now*. Which is an eye-wateringly small number of people. When you look at most marketing and advertising through that prism, you realise why it's so bloody hard to get customers.

When the majority of businesses are competing for the tiny number of buyers who are ready to buy at that exact moment, you get into a bun fight. That's fine for the guy with the biggest wallet; not so good for anyone else in the fight. When there's so much competition, you pay more to compete and have to work harder to attract a buyer confused by choice.

But what if you could shift your message so you didn't have to wrestle in the mud with everyone else? What if you could talk to your ideal buyers and followers long before they ever get to the point of buying, so that when they *do* buy, you're the only one on their mind? And what if you could build such an unassailable relationship with your audience that when it comes to buying, your competition would be rendered irrelevant? Sounds pretty damn hot, right?

That's why you need a better, more compelling cult message.

It's not a USP

Your message is not a USP; it's more than that. If you've heard of this term (it means 'unique selling point', if by any chance you haven't), you probably know exactly what I'm going to say. But ask yourself: have you actually worked on your USP? Do you think your USP is based on one of the following?

- Convenience

- Customer service

- Price.

If your USP is based on one of those, I don't blame you. We've been conditioned to think that convenience, service and price are serious points of difference to customers.

These are not the makings of a cult message. Doing something well is not a central message – in fact, basic competence is not a USP at all, unless you're the best.

Saying 'We're the cheapest supermarket' or 'We are the highest rated business in our sector' can be a USP. But it doesn't make for the kind of message that will allow you to start and build a cult.

In fact, when you get this right, you don't need a USP. Say what, Jody? But isn't having a USP the most important thing in business? Won't my business fail without it?

It will fail if you're marketing and selling your business the traditional way. (And, yes, I am using 'traditional' in a totally derogatory way.) You're competing in a crowded market with little elbow room for anyone else. What I show you in this book is how to step outside of what every other business and brand is doing. By doing this, you build a message that attracts devotees who only have eyes for you. You never need worry again about the competition.

And your USP will be the one thing your competitors will *never* be able to compete against. Your USP will be you, your story and how you grow your cult. And, to me, that's the best goddamn USP anyone can have.

EXAMPLE

THE RYANAIR MESSAGE

Ryanair stands out from the hundreds of other budget airlines because it broadcasts one message above any other: 'We believe customers don't want or care about the unnecessary frills and choose to travel for as little as they can possibly pay.'

Ryanair may not have this message as a slogan on any of its ads, but it is clear from everything the brand does– from its press announcements to every moment CEO Michael O'Leary speaks about the company. It is often regarded as contempt for its customers or lack of care, yet the brand remains as popular as ever. It knows its position and its message.

It's not a mission, purpose or vision

In the last few years, we've suffered very badly from a major pandemic. Many have fallen to this sickness as the infection has spread so rapidly, unchecked for so long. Some don't even know they're affected, and many don't understand the long-term damage caused. I am, of course, talking about the sickness of purpose-itis.

Now, I'm from Brighton, so I'm well aware of how easy it can be to get caught up in pseudo-hippie BS; heck, I even wear vegan sandals most of the time. But the spread of vision and purpose workshops in place of the hard work of formulating a real message is seriously damaging the health of brands.

Yes, it can be great fun to sit around on beanbags, sipping lattes and brainstorming what your company's mission or purpose should be. It really can. It can genuinely inspire you as a team and motivate you in your role. But the truth is, it does nothing to attract people to you – as a message should do.

The problem with so much of this work done by agencies and marketing departments the world over is that it's so inward looking; in trying to set themselves apart, the first place these brands run to is thinking about what they want or what inspires them. This is almost the opposite of what the message needs to be. What they really need to focus on is what message would inspire potential customers.

One of the arguments many people pose against this standpoint is to repeat Simon Sinek's assertion that 'why' is more powerful than 'what'. Sinek's excellent book *Start With Why* is highly recommended, but many have taken it as gospel for only thinking about the why.

Expressing your 'why' can be a differentiator when you are in a market where everyone has the same message. It can set you apart because it establishes an emotional tether to your product or service. Emotion is good. That's what we're shooting for.

But if your message is not compelling or focused on your audience, they won't care. If they don't believe you can help them, explaining your 'why' won't change a thing. The same goes for your vision, your mission or your purpose. It may be a rallying point, yet it doesn't effectively cleave an audience for or against you.

Here's an example. I've seen brands that believe their message is something like the following:

- 'Our goal is to help 100,000 entrepreneurs in the next 10 years' (mission).

- 'We will work to end the ordeal of cancer and improve survival rates for women' (purpose).

- 'We believe that technology is a force for good and every child should have access' (vision).

On the face of it, those are some pretty strong messages. Dig deeper and it becomes clear they aren't messages at all. They're hopes, dreams and goals. They are wonderful expressions of objectives or a direction. But they are not the kind of message that will deliver the following or the strong relationships that build a cult.

These messages probably all look familiar to you. They could be statements made by any coaching company, cancer charity or tech business. They are not polarising; no one is going to disagree with lofty goals for helping children, and no one is pro-cancer. These messages have mass appeal and, as a result, have little power.

Remember, the approaches above do have appeal. These messages can drive followers and fans and attract people around a goal, cause or movement. What they will not do is build a cult.

That's why it's important for you to consider whether you're committed to building a cult. Most leaders, at this point, choose to go back to following the traditional path. They choose mass appeal and keep it broad enough to not rock any boats.

Your mission, vision or purpose cannot be a replacement for creating a message. No amount of hours spent workshopping to figure out any of these things will win you extra followers. Only focusing on your cult message will deliver the strength of feeling and devotion needed to start and grow your cult.

What a message is

So, if it's not your USP or your mission, vision or purpose, what the hell is your message?

Your message is about one thing and one thing only: positioning. By positioning, I mean how your message and your brand fit within your followers' view of the world.

Your central message is what makes your audience want to listen to you. It's the signal beacon around which you start recruiting followers to your cause. Think of it as the message that makes your perfect follower sit up and take notice. It needs to be that compelling.

To make this simple, we can distil it to one question.

The question

Without a compelling answer to this question, you'll not only struggle to build your cult— you'll also hit the buffers trying to attract the attention of possible cult followers. And if no one ever even notices you exist, congratulations: you're the leader of a cult of *one*. Loserville.

Here is the question: **Why should someone join your cult over doing anything else?**

Notice the subtleties of that question (and I freely admit that this book is short on subtleties).

The question isn't about why someone should join your cult over another cult or another group. It's about why they should join your cult over doing *anything else*— including the biggest competitor you'll ever experience: doing nothing.

Yep, you have to compete against lethargy, boredom, apathy and lack of interest. It's a formidable foursome that few brands overcome.

You see, your followers have busy lives. They receive thousands of marketing messages every day. They have emails, text messages and all kinds of social media to distract them. They have everything else going on in their lives.

As much as we want them to focus on our message, we have to be realistic. They have bigger priorities.

They have kids. They have jobs. They have massive fucking pandemics to deal with. That's why your cult message needs to be so clear, compelling and polarising that it cuts right through everything else they are doing or thinking about or dealing with. It needs to cut to the core of where they are right now. And it needs to answer the question: why you? And why now?

THE COMPONENTS OF A CULT MESSAGE

To understand how to do this, we need to look at these individual attributes:

1. Polarising

2. Compelling

3. Clear.

Combine all three and you will see the powerful effect upon your ability to attract, recruit and build your relationship with your cult followers.

Let's break each one down.

1. Polarising

Do you have customers or clients who are an unmitigated pain in the ass? (Like I need to ask…)

You know the ones I'm talking about. The customers who are cheap as hell but can't help sucking every moment of your time.

The nightmare followers who comment on everything and always have to have the last word. Or the entitled freebie-grabbers who take, take, take then bitch and moan when you try to earn an honest dollar from your work.

Those guys.

But what about the customers who love anything and everything you do? They're easy-going, fun to work with, they never quibble about money and they give purpose to what you do. More of those, please!

Imagine how it would feel to have a brand that attracted more of those dream clients and fewer a-holes. It's why having a cult is so powerful. You become magnetic.

A lot has been written and said about brands, products and ideas that are magnetic. It's a compelling idea. You build a brand so attractive that people are uncontrollably drawn towards it. Who wouldn't want that?

Yet there's one aspect most marketing and business books miss about the magnet analogy. A magnet has two poles: one that attracts and one that repels.

Being 'magnetic' isn't solely about attracting people towards you; it's just as important to repel those people who are not a great fit. Because a *great* fit is what we're looking for. Yes, you'll have the painful a-holes who cause all the problems. Most likely, you'll also have followers who are OK – but just OK. They're an adequate fit, but nothing more or less. They don't moan about you openly, but neither do they praise you. They are… nice. Ewww.

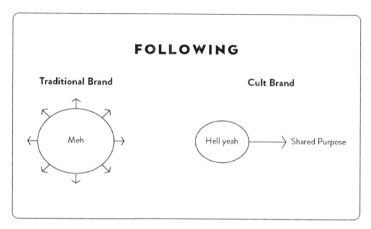

The traditional way of thinking is that your customer base is made up of a mix of these types. A few a-holes, a few fanatics and the majority happy customers. That's one way to run a business or grow a brand. But it's no way to build a cult.

2. Compelling

The word 'compelling' is frustrating. It's one of those words everyone uses without ever defining it. It's like 'dynamic'– used a lot, but understood little.

In this context, I want you to think of it as meaning overwhelming or irresistible to the reader (i.e. potential follower). When they read a compelling message, they know they need it. It invokes a powerful desire.

Getting clear on this definition adds to your understanding of what you need to include. If we want to invoke a desire, it helps to know what your followers ultimately want. 'Ultimately' is the operative word here.

Let's be specific. One mistake brands make in figuring out their customers' desires is thinking too narrowly. Say the brand sells widgets; in this exercise, they would say their customers' desire is to buy a widget. This may be true for a tiny percentage of their potential customer base who are looking to buy a widget at that very moment. You have to be there at the right time to sell to them when they act on their desire. If you try to sell them a widget at any other time, though, your message will fall on deaf ears. The majority of people aren't buying what the majority of businesses are selling at any one time.

In fact, this is why most marketing fails – it tries to sell to people who are not ready or even willing to buy. That's why we want to focus on our customers' broader desires. And to do that, we have to look at a drill.

How to understand what your followers really want

How can a drill help you understand how to sound, act or be compelling? Here's how.

Consider a drill manufacturer trying to understand its customer. The first-level desire is that their customers want to buy a drill. Obvious, right?

But is that really what they want? Do they actually want a drill, or do they want to do something with the drill? Drill a hole, perchance? When someone buys a drill, they don't necessarily want to own a drill, but they do want to drill a hole in a wall. That's a second level.

But can we go deeper than that? Sure. They don't really just want a hole in a wall. They want to do something with the hole in the wall. Hang a picture, maybe. That's the next level.

And then you can ask yourself, why does that person want to hang a picture on their wall? To make their house look nice? To remind them of relatives, friends or happy experiences? Or some other underlying reason? That is the next level.

And, going on, why do they want to feel happy, have a nice house, and so on? It's usually something to do with how they want to feel or a projection of their status. We could go on, but hopefully this makes the point.

(If you're a copywriter or have done any work on separating features and benefits of a product, you're likely to know the story of the drill and the hole already. Often, it stops at the picture and doesn't go any deeper. For the purposes of this exercise, we can keep going.)

You can sell the features (the drill has this many speeds, drill bits included etc.) or benefits (quickly hang the pictures you love, make your house beautiful etc.). So you can see that even if you're a drill manufacturer selling drills, you have many ways to appeal to your customers' desires.

Understand your future cult devotees' ultimate desires by digging deep. When you know what they truly want and desire, you have the tools to craft the perfect cult message.

Remember, it may not always be wanting something; their ultimate desire may be to avoid some pain or problem. You just need to dig.

3. Clear

There is a direct correlation between clarity and virality. The clearer and simpler your message, the easier it is to repeat.

If you want more sales, get clearer on your message. If you want more attention, get clearer on your message. If you want more referrals, get clearer on your message.

The distance your message will travel is proportionate to how simple and how easy to understand and share it is. If you distil your message into a few simple words, it's more likely to be used in its original form in the mouths of others. That's something Silicon Valley start-ups know very well.

These start-ups are constantly pitching for multimillion-dollar investment and so they need to nail their pitch. And the quicker and cleaner they can put across their concept to investors, the better their chances of investment.

That's why you'll hear a barrage of similes whenever you're around start-ups. Everything seems to be the 'Netflix of ——', the 'Amazon of ——' or the 'Airbnb of ——' because similes communicate a subscription, retail or booking model quickly and easily. For example, Rent the Runway is described as the 'Netflix of high fashion'. In just four words, they communicate that this brand applies a subscription model to renting fashion pieces. Pretty simple, eh?

While I don't suggest you take the same approach, think about how you can use analogies or stories to help your listener or reader to understand your ideas instantly.

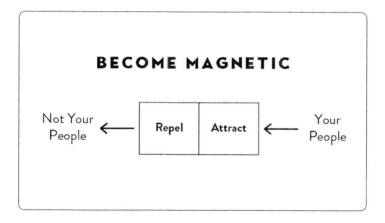

You need to shift your message so that you only attract the fanatics and potential fanatics. How?

Here's the bad news. All those a-holes, pains in the ass and tricky customers are your fault. Every single one of them is in your sphere because you attracted them.

Whether you meant to or not, you have drawn them towards your brand. Your message – or lack of message – has delivered the people you have today. Your message – or lack of message – may have also repelled the exact followers, clients and customers you do want.

Change your message, and you change your following.

The good news is that now you're aware, you can do something about it. Flip the script and craft a message that is magnetic.

When you perfect your message, your brand becomes magnetic to the right followers. The right followers rallying around your message will be more devoted, more vocal and more willing to recruit others. You will develop a deeper, more meaningful connection. Being a devotee of your brand becomes part of their identity.

EXAMPLE

THE BAD BOY RUNNING MESSAGE

The best way to see how this all fits together is with an example from BBR:

The message

Running isn't dull, so why are all its podcasts? We take a look at the side of running no one talks about. BBR is a podcast and community that isn't afraid to laugh at running and you.

Why it works

- It's polarising. A lot of runners *do* like boring stats and running chat and talking about PBs and knocking 10 seconds off their 10k… God, I was losing the will to live just writing that. But that's what some runners like. And it's going to yank their chain to think we've pushed them into the 'boring' category.

- It's compelling. It attracted a vast swathe of runners who wanted to chat about running, but not to have the kinds of conversations that went through the existing running media, websites and podcasts. They wanted a conversation that was more authentic from two people who were more like them (seriously, how helpful are Mo's top tips for hitting your best 1500m time?).

> - It's clear. In a few sentences, you understand exactly what we're about. This clarity makes it easy for our followers to repeat the message to others.
>
> As you can see, your cult message doesn't need to be complicated. But it does have to be well thought out. Your cult message must create distance between you and others in your market.

When you understand the value of the cult message, you see it everywhere. I've avoided talking about the big global brands that you see every other business and marketing book use, like Tesla, Apple and Virgin. But each of these has a clear central message if you look – and those messages are simple, clear and easy to articulate.

EXERCISE

FIGURE OUT YOUR COMPETITORS' MESSAGES

There are three parts to this exercise and it takes a little bit of research. But I guarantee, it'll open your eyes to the opportunity in your market.

Make a list of all the businesses and brands in your market. Starting with their website, go through and pick out what the key messages are that they're communicating. What is the main message they communicate first? Can you tell exactly who they are trying to appeal to? How do they communicate what makes them unique? What benefits do they lead with? Once you've looked at their website, move on to looking at all the other places they post content or advertise. Do they carry the message from their website consistently? Or do they have different messages?

Do this for all of your competitors. You may already start to see some patterns or themes. How similar or different are the messages communicated by your competition? Are they same-y or do they vary wildly?

The next step is to judge how well their message stands up to the three components of a cult message:

1. Is it polarising? Does it actually force the reader to make an in/out choice?

2. Is it compelling? Does it provoke a strong desire in the target audience?

3. Is it clear? Is it simple to understand and easy to repeat?

It's not easy hitting a 'yes' on all three. This exercise will show you how well your competition is doing and throw some light on whether your current message is up to scratch.

This is also a great exercise to do with brands you admire or want to be more like. You'll see how well they hit the mark on these points.

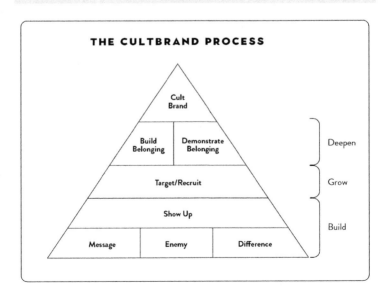

THE CULTBRAND PROCESS

- Cult Brand
- Build Belonging | Demonstrate Belonging — Deepen
- Target/Recruit — Grow
- Show Up
- Message | Enemy | Difference — Build

When you do this, you discover why messages either work or don't. It helps to dissect messaging in this way and makes it easier when it's your turn.

GET INVOLVED

Want more examples of cult messaging from other brands? Sign up to the 'How to Start a Cult' mini-course and receive more case studies to help when crafting your own cult message. Register for free here: **www.cultbrandmethod.com**

HOW TO START CRAFTING YOUR MESSAGE

I've shown you why you need a strong cult message to attract and grow your following. You've also seen why so many brands get it wrong and struggle to build a message with the power to grow a following. Now it's over to you.

EXERCISE

WHAT SETS YOU APART?

Building a polarising cult message is not about being pointlessly contrarian. Disagreeing with everything is not a strategy; you often end up coming across as ranty and angry. You don't need to do this to be polarising.

To be polarising, you need to hold a view that is different from others in your industry. The first step of building your message is identifying what that view could be.

A good place to start is to focus on industry or market 'givens'. These are ideas, concepts or beliefs that people take for granted. Ask yourself:

•   What does everyone else in your sector believe?

•   What common assumptions are held up as true?

•   What is everyone else telling your future followers they should be doing?

Another good starting point is focusing on issues your sector is facing that could affect your future followers. Use your own knowledge and experience to answer these questions:

- What is everyone talking about?

- What is no one talking about that they should be talking about?

- What problems/pains/challenges are being ignored by others?

By identifying what other companies are doing right now, you can more clearly see gaps no one is occupying. By flipping those questions on their head, you can start to see the outlines of possible cult messages:

- Can you say something that everyone else is afraid to say?

- Can you say something that goes against the accepted wisdom?

- Can you challenge a belief that everyone else is reluctant to challenge?

Say something that sets you apart from everyone else, and people will sit up and take notice. Here are some examples.

If you're in the fitness niche, it may be declaring that counting calories makes you fat. It may be saying that too much aerobic exercise is bad for you.

If you're in the automotive industry, it may be highlighting why buying new car regs is crazy and why you should wait four months.

It could be anything that is counter to what your audience are likely to have heard before. The important part is: you have to genuinely believe it as well. Otherwise, you're a fraud.

Ask yourself:

- Which of your beliefs puts you in a minority in your industry?

- What do you believe that no one else believes?

- What is different about your approach?

Remember, you want to stand out – but you also want to win over your new cult devotees.

Polarisation is as much about empathy as it is about attention. You have to polarise, but you also have to be on your followers' side.

Sure, you're going to lose people who don't align with your message. That's the hardest pill to swallow if you're not used to it. But the payout is followers who love the fact you're out there talking about the frustrations they feel and have 'entered the conversation already going on in their head'.

EXERCISE

WHAT IS YOUR MESSAGE?

By now you should have some ideas, either in your head or written down. It's time to start creating your cult message.

Try bringing together what you discovered above. It really helps when drafting these to use complete sentences. There are a few sentence starters below that will help formulate your thoughts:

- Every other business in my sector believes ——, but that is wrong because ——.

- Every business/brand tells customers to ——.

- Most consumers think they should ——, but what they really need to do is ——.

Juxtaposing current or existing beliefs or ideas with your polarising or contrary thoughts provides a starting point. Getting your message isn't a two-minute job; it will take time.

Try drafting 10–15 different statements, choose three that really resonate with you and maybe share them with your team or colleagues.

GET INVOLVED

Better still, head on over to the Cult Leader Facebook group and post your cult message ideas so your fellow cult leaders can give feedback. Go to: **www.facebook.com/groups/ howtostartacult**

SUMMARY

In this chapter, you discovered that:

- Your message is key to attracting new followers, repelling disbelievers and reinvigorating momentum.

- Followers are more likely to post, engage, create and share when they have clear parameters.

- Most brands don't have a message – and those that do exist don't work. A perfect polarising message is clear, creates contrast and energises your followers.

- A strong message has to answer the question 'Why choose to join this cult over every other option?'

- The path to a perfect message lies in understanding what your followers desire. It needs to separate your brand in their mind from other brands.

THOU SHALT PICK AN ENEMY

Every fairy tale needs a good villain.

JIM MORIARTY, SHERLOCK

In this chapter, I show you:

- Why you need to pick your enemies

- How to hack directly into your followers' emotions (in a good way)

- What everyone gets wrong about choosing enemies (or why having enemies is not about throwing rocks)

- How to pick the right enemies to energise and enthuse your cult devotees.

"

No cult can grow
without an enemy

"

WHY YOU NEED AN ENEMY

Now, why would you want your business to have enemies? Surely that's exactly the opposite of what you want?

In this chapter, I want to show you that defining and identifying your enemy isn't just important; it is *essential* if you're going to achieve cult-like status. On the face of it, the approach appears aggressive and counterintuitive. But dig a little deeper and you discover why it's the only way to build a cult.

Every cult needs an opposing force: an external enemy against which the cult leader and their followers can rally.

Think about all the great stories, fables and myths that have captured human imagination. What do they all have in common? Great bad guys (or girls). Jim Moriarty was right.

From Beowulf's Grendel to Captain Hook, from Voldemort to Thanos, the villain of the piece always seems to steal the show. Part of this is down to emotion. The villain who represents injustice, unfairness or any other bending of the way we want the world to be provides a rallying point, because they irk us, raise our ire and cause a welling up of emotion. The ability to raise your blood pressure is why invoking an enemy is so powerful, and why authors, playwrights and screenwriters lean so heavily on them. Well, it's high time to steal their secrets and deploy this in service of building your cult.

No cult can grow without an enemy. It's the linchpin upon which everything else hangs. The value of an enemy cannot be overstated.

Without an enemy or villain, your cult doesn't have a focal point for its energy – at least at the start. The villain is a rallying point. In fact, it's *the* rallying point.

Trying to grow a cult another way will result in failure. No cult could survive without this vital piece of the puzzle. Ignore this and you won't win the attention of the right kind of followers: those who have the potential to become devoted cult members. By picking the right villain, you can attract exactly the right followers – and plenty of them.

Villains offer an opportunity for them to engage and contribute, and to build connection with other cult members by coming together around a common foe. Achieving this without an enemy as the focal point takes longer, costs more and is never as effective.

On the other hand, choosing the right kind of enemy for your cult can rapidly build your following. By rallying against their foe, you make them feel like you are speaking for them. They feel someone understands. And it connects with them on an emotional level that cuts all the way through other distractions.

Enemies will give you content, internal loyalty and a way of channelling the cult's energy.

FIND THE ENEMIES THAT DEFINE YOUR GROUP

The reason why so many groups and wannabe cults fail to take hold isn't related to their reach. You can burn a wedge of cash building an audience of people who like your message and will follow you. Doesn't cost them a thing. It generates a false sense of security, though. That reach doesn't always translate to actual influence.

And being the leader of a gang of people who don't listen to you or give a shit about your thoughts… well, it's like being a parent. Thankless, painful and leaving you wondering why you bothered in the first place.

The real key to developing influence is engagement and deepening the connection you have with your audience. Bring the right people into the fold and build a relationship with them in the right way, and that meaningful connection turns into meaningful influence.

Empathy is your weapon here (but not in a touchy-feely, let-me-rub-your-back-and-put-Enya-on-Spotify way). You signal empathy by siding with your followers against a common enemy.

If you help others – particularly those who are vulnerable or feel like they're not heard – to attack a common foe, you will win them to your side.

In dangerous cults, this is a very common trait and a key method to manipulate and turn cult followers against the rest of the world. The 'us versus them' dynamic is one of the most important methods for indoctrinating and keeping people locked into cults, against their best interests. Obviously, I'm not going to recommend using the idea of enemies or villains to manipulate your audience in this way.

However, it's worth stepping back and trying to understand why this works so well on cult followers. The reason why throwing rocks at enemies, vilifying outsiders and pointing fingers at others holds such power to engage and stir the emotions comes back to psychology.

EXAMPLE

BAD BOY RUNNING VERSUS CYCLISTS

Defining enemies was undoubtedly key to the growth of BBR. We had in our target people who take running too seriously, who are too competitive and are knee-deep in their running club, but our one key enemy, the one that really captured the imagination, was cyclists.

Importantly, we express our antipathy in a humorous and light-hearted way. This isn't that douchey all-bikes-should-be-banned-from-the-road belief, but more an acknowledgement that cycling is much easier than running – hence, cyclists are official cheats in BBR land. Having this clearly defined and publicised regularly has three effects:

1. It's a rallying point for our cult members that grabs their attention. Cyclists are a divisive issue for many of the runners in our community. It was clear when we outlined our stance that there was an emotional reaction to it. We weren't overly worried that any cyclists in the group would find it offensive, mainly because it

was clear upon entry to the group there was something around cyclists when they joined.

2. It rapidly grew the group and generated discussion with the right followers.

3. It allows cult followers to understand how to interact within the group. Within weeks of the Facebook group launching, members were independently posting using our stated 'enemies' as inspiration. We'd set parameters for their interaction within which they could contribute.

We're not afraid to speak out against the enemies. You need to be the same. Not only does throwing rocks at your enemies attract new followers who wish to do the same, it gives voice to those in your cult and beyond if you articulate their concerns/worries/possibilities for them. It builds connection with you; they get heard.

Defining an enemy makes it obvious that this is either the place for a potential follower or it isn't. It's clear. There is no grey area. Now, the interesting thing about BBR is that many in our community are cyclists as well; in fact, there's no way we could grow unless we appealed to both groups. But, as a cyclist, you either have a sense of humour to see the enemy as funny (in which case, you're one of us) or you get upset by it and don't find it funny (in which case, the community simply isn't for you). As you will see as we move through the book, at every point we're 'qualifying' our followers, giving them opportunities to continually opt in or opt out if it's not right for them. The people who end up in your cult should be there because they actively opted in at every stage. Let the disbelievers fall by the wayside. You only want true devotees.

Your goal with the cult is to only attract those who are really devoted. And it begins with picking enemies.

This can feel counterintuitive and negative in the beginning, but I assure you this feeling will pass once you see the possibilities. Remember, this is about empathy, not antipathy towards others. You identify enemies to show you are on the side of your followers.

When I start working with brands, another common objection is 'We don't have any enemies'. On the surface, it may seem like you don't have any enemies, or that you only have one or two. But I want you to dig deeper. When I go through this process with brands and businesses, it often starts off with head-scratching and doubt that this is possible. But take your time to unlock this and you'll soon get into the flow.

I worked directly with a global Buddhism brand on their message, and we did this exercise. When we first started discussing the idea of identifying 'villains', they were adamant that there were either none or very few in their industry. After 10 minutes of unlocking the conversation, however, I was struggling to keep up with their ideas on the whiteboard. Every business has villains and enemies. If Buddhists can come up with enemies, you most certainly can, too.

After reading this you may have switched off and dismissed the idea as unworkable. Many people will tell themselves this is all well and good, but it won't work with their brand. They will rationalise their way out of committing to this action. If that sounds like you, put this book down now. You're not going to have the stomach for everything else you need to do in the coming chapters. And that's fine, because this approach requires commitment to all the stages; if there's any doubt in your mind, it will be difficult to bring others along. If you do stick with this approach, though, I guarantee you will stand out in your sector, quickly build a following of devotees and watch as they grow your cult for you.

HOW THE PSYCHOLOGY WORKS

An enemy is a powerful emotional driver because the hero–villain dynamic is so simple. It makes a choice black and white. You're either with the villain or you're with the hero. If you're clearly on the side of the hero, there's a certainty you're good, too. And we like certainty and feeling good about ourselves for, well, feeling good.

In other words, having a well-defined villain or enemy puts a clear line down. You're either with us or against us. Or, put another way, if you're not part of the solution, you're part of the problem. You know whose side you're on.

As much as nuance makes a tale thought-provoking and ultimately more intellectually satisfying, it doesn't provoke the same acute emotional response as a clear-cut, pure evil villain. (Attempts by popular movie franchises to bring more complexity to bad guys have fallen flat with cinema audiences for good reason. Ahem... Bond.)

Yes, we love a good villain, but we always want to know we're going to get a happy ending and the villain ultimately will be defeated.

An enemy also offers a way of abdicating self-responsibility. This sounds horrible written down, but done the right way, it makes people feel empowered.

It feels empowering to have the responsibility for your circumstances lifted off your shoulders by blaming someone other than yourself for the situation you find yourself in.

Time and again we see how brands, movements and organisations hold up a scapegoat to blame for some major problem. This approach has a long and varied history. On one side of the British political spectrum, we see politicians using the EU, immigrants, 'wokeness' and the BBC as punching bags to rally their base. On the other, we see the blame put on Tories, cronyism, Thatcher (still), austerity and Little Englander-ism.

In a more constructive way, we also see consumer champions vilifying banks and insurance companies, and health experts turning the blame on food corporations for our terrible national diet.

Telling your followers and audience that the negative aspects of their lives aren't their own fault, in whatever way, can elevate your position.

Remember, the most important driver behind why enemies get people engaged is that you demonstrate empathy. By aligning with the enemies of your enemies, you win over more friends.

People want to feel connected and heard. Get it right, talk to their issues and problems – and the people, companies and practices that cause them – and your cult will flourish.

Uniting the tribe against a common enemy brings together an audience that may not necessarily share a common vision, and ultimately helps the growth and expansion of your cult.

What it isn't

- This isn't about bitching about your competitors.

- This isn't about coming across as a sore loser, or jealous.

- And it's not about mob rule.

I certainly don't want you to go out and start torching or bad-mouthing other businesses. The point about choosing an enemy or two to rail against is nothing to do with singling out individuals or businesses. This isn't about demonising individuals, or bullying in any way. Not only is that bad for your brand, it also makes you a very naughty person. Don't do it. The last thing you want is to be part of an online mob gone crazy against someone.

You're not looking to find an enemy to direct your followers against. You are not trying to get people to respond negatively to something they may be neutral about. This is about drawing out something that is already frustrating them.

What it is

When you identify common enemies, right away you give your followers subjects and ideas around which to rally. The enemy doesn't necessarily need to be product related; in fact, it's better if it isn't.

A good strong cult message can elevate your product or service, or yourself as a campaigning brand. For example, Jamie Oliver wasn't promoting his cookbook or restaurants when he was campaigning for better school meals. But neither was he blaming the dinner ladies or the school for the situation. Instead, he smartly made an enemy of the Turkey Twizzler. This was a perfect enemy because it embodied all the problems with school dinners without placing the blame on anyone.

Identifying an enemy or two has a couple of key functions for the purpose of growing your cult:

1. It allows people to clearly and easily identify whether they fit within the group.

2. It allows people within the group to clearly and easily rail, protest or pontificate about something they know will resonate with other group members.

This is about empathy. You want to collude with your followers, not inspire them to bullying or violence.

An enemy can be many things, including:

A person

There may be an individual who personifies all that is wrong with the world. They are likely to be a well-known name to your cult followers, someone who inspires an emotional reaction. That personal grudge you have against Mabel at the Post Office is unlikely to inspire your cult; an individual who is perceived as responsible for the challenges facing your sector or your cult followers is better. Certain political leaders prove to be rallying points, such as Obama and Hillary for US Republicans, or Trump for everyone else. For it to be a person, they normally have to be very well known.

A company

There may be one company that stands out in your sector as the source of frustration or anger for your followers. It may also be your major rival, although it's more likely to be a dominant, almost monopolistic company in an industry – one that throws its weight around because of its size, or represents an 'old way' of doing things.

For example, if you're an independent bookseller, the enemy is likely to be Amazon and everything it stands for. It's likely you'd be able to rally other booksellers around that level of pariah.

An organisation

The enemy may not be a company, but an organisation. Many a crazy cult leader has rallied their followers against hidden or shadowy organisations that threatened their way of life or were 'really in control'. It's quite surprising to hear how many people genuinely believe in conspiracy theories of supranational cabals pulling the strings of world politics. We probably don't need to stray into that territory, but there may be organisations that do rile your followers. In the US, liberals vilify the National Rifle Association as representing everything bad about the country. Equally, conservatives rail against Planned Parenthood as an attack on their values. Who do your cult followers see as a threat to their future?

A practice

The enemy may not be a tangible entity, but an industry practice that is hated by your followers. For example, for savers an enemy may be income tax payable on savings. For homebuyers, two enemies may be gazumping, or paying stamp duty. For mobile phone users, it may be early release clauses in contracts. Each sector, profession and industry has its villainous practices which are greater for rallying your cause around.

A practice is a particularly effective enemy, as it allows you to avoid directly attacking an individual person, company or organisation.

EXAMPLE

NETFLIX VERSUS BLOCKBUSTER

A great example here is Netflix and its path to winning over followers.

Netflix was a thorn in Blockbuster's side. But in the early days, it was careful about its relationship with Blockbuster. Netflix could have directly attacked its competitor brand, but it knew Blockbuster's audience and what would resonate with others who weren't part of that audience. It knew that if you were a film buff or geek, you were probably already renting VHSs and DVDs. And if you were, you most likely used Blockbuster. And the one big thing everyone hated about Blockbuster was its late fees.

Rather than focus its ire directly on Blockbuster, which was still a much-loved brand at the time, Netflix focused on late fees. It was clever. Late fees were hated but made up a large part of Blockbuster's revenue. By bringing the issue to the fore, Netflix could win rental fans to its side without actively calling for the end of Blockbuster. Attack their revenue stream and let your followers do your bidding.

Beliefs

There may be a dominant belief in your sector that you want to counter, and against which your followers can rally. A good belief enemy is one to which your own approach runs counter.

An example would be a belief that a job should be performed a certain way, such as journalists remaining neutral in their reporting or doctors maintaining a professional distance from patients. It could be the belief that a product should be purchased in a defined way, such as that high-street fashion, make-up or furniture needs to be tried and tested in store before purchase. It may be a belief that people should apply criteria for buying or acting that are counter to what you believe.

It could also be a broader belief, one that isn't specific to an industry. You may rally your followers against beliefs that represent different sides of their dominant values. You can just as easily make an enemy of traditional thinking – 'we've always done it this way' – as you can of progressive thinking – 'we need to rip it up and start again'.

Attitudes

There may be a prevailing attitude that raises the hackles of your followers. These may be attitudes like, 'I'm alright, Jack', 'It'll sort itself out' or 'Someone else will deal with it'. It may be an attitude of indifference towards followers because of who they are, or an attitude of aggression or persecution. For example, you may rail against outdated or persistent attitudes towards sexuality, stereotypes, societal norms or anything that is deeply connected to your audience. Either way, attitudes can be a powerful enemy.

Behaviours

Certain behaviours can also be the enemy. Remember, not all enemies are external; enemies can also be undesirable traits and behaviours your followers want to rid themselves of but cannot, such as apathy or envy. Maybe procrastination or paralysis in the face of action is one of the most frustrating behaviours for your followers. It is internal– but it's an enemy, nonetheless. These enemies can be more powerful than external factors because they are so pervasive and felt on an hour-by-hour basis.

Character traits

It may even be a character trait or emotion that you see as the enemy standing in between where your followers are and where they want to go. This can be anything from fear or selfishness to greed or impatience. They may be traits your own followers are frustrated with in themselves, or character traits in others that your followers rail against.

Annoyances

The enemy may be something as quibbling as annoyances. Enough minor annoyances, drip-fed to anyone over a period of time, will develop into a major enemy. Think parking tickets; on the face of it, not a major problem. But these minor annoyances sometimes take on the status of representing something else. The innocuous parking ticket may symbolise different things to different individuals: another way for the government to take money off the ordinary person, a loss of freedom, a move away from the good old days when parking was free and plentiful (nostalgia), or a reflection back on to them of their lack of self-discipline or timekeeping. Small things quickly become big things and make perfect enemies around which to rally others.

WHAT MAKES A 'GOOD' ENEMY?

Not all enemies are created equal. Picking the wrong enemy has consequences. At best, you'll fail to attract the right – or any – followers to your cult. At worst, you can seriously damage your reputation and set your cause back. Choosing your enemy or enemies requires thought. A good enemy has to be:

- Someone or something that provokes a negative response in your audience. It must be a pre-existing issue they have, rather than one you have engineered.

- Something that other people haven't called out, or an original way of calling out an enemy that has been identified before.

- On your followers' radar and an active and present enemy. It has to have consequences that are felt.

Let's come back to this point: it's not about you. The enemy of your cult isn't your biggest competitor, or something or someone you're personally against. The purpose of choosing an enemy is to demonstrate empathy and connection to your followers. You have to choose the enemies that are *their* enemies.

It may be the case that they are also your enemies; in fact, most of the time this will be true. At some point, you were in your customers' shoes. You know what they're going through. The thing you saw as an enemy then may still be the same. If there was a Zen-like way of saying this: your enemies should align. Those are the perfect enemies.

EXERCISE

FIND YOUR CULT'S/AUDIENCE'S ENEMIES

You may not have a clue right now who your cult's enemies are. Or you may already have had one or two dominant, clear enemies in your mind as you've been reading through this.

For this exercise, I want you to go crazy. Your goal is to identify as many potential enemies as you can in each of the categories that resonate with your future cult followers.

Here are the categories of enemy:

- A person

- A company

- An organisation

- A practice

- A belief

- An attitude

- A behaviour

- A character trait

- An annoyance.

This is a great exercise to go through with your team and is particularly useful as you'll really need to dig down into it to mine the gold.

Start by working your way through each category and asking the following questions to generate ideas in relation to each of them:

- Who do your cult followers blame for their situation?

- What is causing your cult followers to continue to be in the situation?

- What or who is stopping them escaping their pain or reaching their desire?

List out all the enemies that cause an issue in your industry or sector. Write down every idea, business, practice and so on that your customers or clients or those who operate suffer from or who are a constant thorn in their side. This exercise is best done on a large sheet of paper or whiteboard so you can quickly scribble down ideas. Don't be vanilla – we want something that provokes an emotional reaction. It doesn't have to be anger. It could be disappointment or frustration. Anything that you think elicits an emotional response from your audience is perfect for this.

At the end of this process, you will have a long list of potential cult enemies.

The next step is to rate them. Do this by identifying which ones provoke the strongest emotional reaction from your potential followers. I call this an 'Emotive Rating'. Give each enemy a score out of 10, with 10 being a 'hot button' for your followers that sends them over the edge at the mere mention of the enemy.

You may not be 100% sure at this stage, but do it and keep it rough.

The final step is to eliminate those enemies that score less than an eight. If they don't provoke an acute emotional response, get rid and store them up for later if you need them. You should now have a list of enemies ready to rile your followers.

WARNING: Only go through this process with others who have bought into this cult-building process. This is hard to understand for those who haven't, and there will be resistance if they don't fully get it. We've been so indoctrinated into believing we need to be everything to all people. But you're being the leader. You're doing something different that will make you really stand out. Remember, small brands that did this turned into big brands. They understood it was the fastest route to building a following. Getting this right strengthens the connection between your followers and yourself or your brand.

GET INVOLVED

Struggling to come up with the right villains for your cult,
or need help narrowing down your list? Join the Cult Leader
Facebook group and share your exercise to get feedback from
other leaders. Go to **www.facebook.com/groups/how-
tostartacult**

SUMMARY

In this chapter, you discovered that:

- Picking an enemy or two is vital to building a deep connection with your cult followers.

- The real key to building influence among your followers is engagement and deepening the relationship.

- Demonstrating empathy and removing self-responsibility for your audience's pain is important.

- Choosing common enemies is important for audiences to rally around.

- Identifying the enemy should not be used to manipulate or kick off bullying behaviour.

- Enemies don't need to be people or companies; they can be practices, beliefs or other intangibles holding followers back.

- When you get this right, you improve your connection, give your followers the tools to contribute, and add an important emotional dimension to your cult.

THOU SHALT BE DIFFERENT. AND CELEBRATE IT

"

Megamind: 'You're a villain alright.
Just not a super one.'
Titan: 'Oh yeah – what's the difference?'
Megamind: 'Presentation!'

MEGAMIND

In this chapter, I show you:

- Why you need to be different and celebrate that fact

- Why different is better than better

- The mistake most brands make when trying to be different

- How to be genuinely different in your market.

Accompanied by the pounding opening guitar riff from Guns N' Roses' 'Welcome to the Jungle', Will Ferrell's blue-headed master villain Megamind swoops into action on a tide of blood-red drones to commence battle.

Megamind was right. Everything is about presentation. No matter how many times he is defeated, he gets back up and shows up in his own unique style – even if it has a whiff of S&M about it. How you show up shapes how your followers see you.

I once sat at a WrestleMania event, watching Lemmy and Motörhead set up for 20 minutes so they could play 'Ace of Spades' for 45 seconds as the entrance music for one of the major stars of WWE.

How much better would life be if your choice of entrance music accompanied your arrival into any room? (I've thought long and hard about this. My entrance music would be Ini Kamoze's 'Here Comes the Hotstepper'.)

How your brand looks, feels and acts is another key factor in attracting and connecting followers to your cult. And that is all about presentation.

"

Fundamentally, you want
to do something very
simple: stand out

"

WHY YOU NEED TO BE DIFFERENT

There aren't many books that discuss cults with respect to brand identity. Funny, that.

You don't expect to see cult leaders sitting on beanbags in a branding agency office, workshopping ideas on Post-it notes and sipping lattes. (Although I wouldn't rule this out in some New York or London agencies.)

As I've said already, I'm no cult academic, but even I'm sure that most cults don't start this way. When you're a charismatic, all-powerful cult leader, you don't do anything by committee.

Fundamentally, you want to do something very simple: stand out.

Coco Chanel knew the power of difference when she said: 'In order to be irreplaceable, one must always be different.'

This is what difference is all about. Think of your brand as though it were a packet of crisps, a box of cereal or another product stacked on a shelf next to all the other businesses and brands your customers could choose. Imagine your customer standing in front of that shelf, looking at all the different products and brands in one go. What would they see? How confident are you that your brand would 'pop' on the shelf? Or would it blend in and get lost among everything else? Your answer to this question determines how hard you need to work on your differentiation.

No matter how strange it sounds, a cult *is* a brand. It has the characteristics of a brand, so it makes sense to look at cults from a brand perspective. If you were a cult leader and you came to my agency looking to build awareness and gain followers, there is a clear starting point.

We've already seen the importance of a cult message, in Chapter 6. A polarising message is one essential element in the arsenal that allows us to reach and attract potential new cult followers. But on its own, it may not be enough. To gain attention with potential cult followers, we need a visceral and obvious point of difference.

This means:

- Looking different

- Sounding different

- Acting different

- Being different.

You need to do this to create distance between your brand and others in your space. Contrast is the single most powerful tool for attracting the attention of those who have never experienced your brand before. For reasons of psychology that we'll explore shortly, new is exciting.

Why different is better than better

Back when I was an entertainment journalist, I interviewed Tom Hardy. It was a short while before he gained megastar status, but

he was still a pretty big name; he was about to start filming for
Mad Max: Fury Road.

When I stepped into the room to speak to him about that next
film role, I didn't know that he was about to hand me a piece of
advice about differentiation that stays with me to this day.

Very early on in his career when he was auditioning against
other actors for a small number of roles, he realised he needed
an edge. He was a good actor, but so was every other actor going
for the same role.

Instead of focusing on the seemingly impossible task of just
becoming an even better actor to try to stand out from the rest,
Hardy took a different approach. He became a body transformation specialist.

He knew that if he worked at it, he could change how he looked
and how his body looked for each of his roles. Watch him in
Bronson or *Inception* or *Venom* and you'll see his look is completely different.

By being different in this way, he got the attention of casting
directors. If you were making a film that required a specific look,
Tom was your guy. Other actors known for this kind of approach
are Christian Bale and Matthew McConaughey.

Rather astutely, Hardy had mastered the important marketing
lesson that, when it comes to standing out, different is better
than better.

To be better than someone else you have to be significantly, immeasurably and perceptibly better. That's a hard thing to show. But being different is simple. You just need to look, act or be different from those around you.

Be more Tom. Be different.

Embracing stark difference is important for your cult when it comes to building belonging and allowing cult members to demonstrate their devotion. A weak brand doesn't translate well to expressions of cult-like devotion in the outside world.

That wise philosopher, Russell Brand, once said that for a person to stand out, you should be able to recognise them by their profile – which presumably explains the backcombed mop he sported for most of his broadcasting career. His thought is spot-on.

Instant recognition as a result of how you look, how you sound and what you say is a powerful tool for gaining and holding attention.

Like the red of Coca-Cola, the shape of a Heinz Tomato Ketchup bottle or McDonald's 'I'm Lovin' It' jingle, you have real brand power when you occupy a sensory space in the mind of your audience.

It works – because that's exactly what we did when we launched the BBR podcast. And it's the same process I successfully use to help brands set themselves apart.

EXAMPLE

BAD BOY RUNNING

Our starting point was what was already out there. As I mentioned earlier in the story, all the other podcasts and communities were either filled with motivational quotes and people telling each other to 'smash it', or focused on technical details like beating your PB. Yawnsville.

We made it clear from the very start that we didn't take running seriously and would celebrate the incapable, give a voice to the non-runner, and venerate those who DNFed (did not finish).

More importantly, we looked and sounded very different, right from the beginning. The way you talk to your audience can immediately differentiate you from your competitors, and so it should be with your cult.

Instead of the usual images of the podcast hosts in their running kit in some heroic pose or as the 'experts', we used images of us in BBR merch, surrounded by beer.

The method we used to set ourselves apart visually as a podcast couldn't be simpler. We checked out what every other podcast in the same category looked like, and picked a bunch of colours and a look that were in stark contrast. And it worked.

Sometimes being different can be as simple as seeing what everyone else is doing and making a different choice.

We were different and we celebrated it.

You've probably heard the phrase 'Marmite brand'– well, that was exactly what we set out to be. We were under no illusions we had broad appeal. You either loved us or you hated us.

We enjoyed a ton of really positive, gushing five-star reviews from listeners who had finally found a home for their running listening – and a big audience of people who weren't even runners, who just enjoyed the chat (yeah, we don't get it either). Crucially, we also got a handful of reviews from listeners who absolutely hated us and what we were doing. They didn't share our values, didn't like our outlook, and felt we should be more professional (and, in my case, should stop talking altogether. Being told not to exist is particularly harsh feedback).

Instead of listening to their feedback and wringing our hands that they weren't our fwends, we embraced the hate. We capitalised on their criticism. We owned it and wore it as war paint. We used it to promote the podcast to an even wider audience, who were curious about why a podcast would use negative reviews to promote itself and about just how bad it could be.

Boring   2y ago

★☆☆☆☆   Daisykinn1

AF

Unpleasant cr*p   3y ago

★☆☆☆☆   pete105

Tried listening to a few episodes and find some bits funny, but so much emphasis on pi55-taking without offering recourse and building a Facebook group of followers trotting out the same rubbish.   more

---

Bad boy, no just bad!   5y ago

★☆☆☆☆   Mike Westwood

Just a pair of idiots giggling like beavus and butthead. Worst running podcast ive ever heard

We printed posters and a banner incorporating the criticism and negative reviews. The more we promoted the hate, the more our real fans loved being part of the kind of cult that celebrated being negged.

Step into your difference and use it to your advantage. Your competitors won't know what to do. And your followers will love it.

WHY CONTRAST WORKS

We're very quickly realising that our belief that humans are sensible beings driven by logic and rational thinking is wholly misguided. We're still very much cavemen and women, driven by our emotions. You can see clear evidence of this in anyone who has had to wait on the customer support line to Virgin Media or been stuck on the M25 when late for a meeting. Even the most rational, balanced person can succumb to blind fury and wild emotion.

Throughout the Cult Commandments, tapping into our cult devotees' emotions is a recurring theme. Here it also plays a part in triggering our monkey brain.

Our brains are simple. They don't really like complexity. When you experience something for the first time, you don't assess it rationally and independently. Your fight, flight or freeze instinct kicks in, and your brain tries to compartmentalise and simplify the situation. If you see something you think you've seen before, your brain files it away in the 'seen that before, it's this…' category.

What really gets our attention and forces us out of our everyday malaise is something we've not seen before. We're hardwired to react to what is different and new.

We also prefer simplicity of choice. Have you ever stood staring at packets of crisps in the snacks aisle of a supermarket? So much choice, so little time. We become wracked with paralysis and confusion when we are faced with too many similar choices. We find it difficult to choose between items of a similar shape, size, colour, design or value.

So the best way to get the attention you want is to create a contrast in your audience's mind that simplifies their decision-making process.

EXAMPLE

THE YELLOW BRIEFCASE

Here is a popular scenario to demonstrate the power of contrast. A man goes for an interview wearing a suit. The other men being interviewed are also wearing suits. (For some reason, this is a pretty misogynist, non-diverse workplace, but bear with me as I make the point.) He has similar experience and expertise to all the other besuited candidates. When the interviewing panel deliberate on the interviewees, their criteria for comparison are experience and expertise. Which is tricky; with so many men in suits with similar experience, the panel must wade through those applications carefully.

Let's change the situation. A man goes for an interview wearing exactly the same as in the first scenario, except for one detail: he takes a yellow briefcase. There is no difference between the man's levels of experience and expertise and everyone else's. However, because he has brought a yellow briefcase, the interviewing panel has a distinct visual clue they associate with him. They cannot – try as they might – disconnect the distinctness of the yellow briefcase from the man. When it comes to comparing interviewees, a contrast has been created that they cannot escape from. There are the people in suits they have interviewed… and there is the man with the yellow briefcase. Regardless of the decision they make, in their minds that man with the yellow briefcase has differentiated himself. It doesn't mean they'll hire him rather than one of the others, just on the basis of having a banana-coloured bag. But it gives him an advantage because he's engineered a contrast, become harder to forget and shifted the criteria for the decision-makers.

Without creating a difference from other cult brands, you cannot stand out. It's impossible. With the thousands of distractions your followers are dealing with every day, only the distinct gains an advantage. By making yourself distinctive, you help followers to make a clear choice between options.

What it isn't

Difference isn't just a gimmick – it has to be meaningful. Superficial difference is seen through right away. Being contrary for the sake of contrariness doesn't wash if you're not actually a contrarian, and neither does trying to convey a sense of humour when you're patently not funny (even if you really, really think you are). The difference has to be authentic to you.

Being different is about transforming the relationship you have with your audience. It is changing the focus on to how you want to make your audience feel.

What it is

Every so often, something comes along that completely flips around what you know about a product or something else you're familiar with. In an instant, you see it in a different light. And you wonder why you never saw it that way before.

The product may not be different. The company selling it may not even be different. The only thing that has changed is the way the company has presented itself. They changed the way they spoke, the way they looked and how they made you feel when you saw what they offered.

When that happens, entire industries can get disrupted, and it gives momentum to the brand that decided to change the game.

Slapping your audience in the face with something so new and different from what they're used to is exciting. And it can even grow you a billion-dollar company.

EXAMPLE

DOLLAR SHAVE CLUB

Dollar Shave Club has a cult following thanks to its difference.

In the machismo world of razor advertising, the likes of Gillette and Wilkinson Sword relied almost exclusively on chiselled chins and ever-growing numbers of blades. Very masculine, very technical and very similar to the way washing powder was advertised – by focusing on features.

Then along came Dollar Shave Club. With just one ad, produced at a fraction of the cost of most Gillette ads, this upstart brand shook the industry to its core.

Yes, it has a polarising message: you shouldn't be paying more than $1 for your blades. But it was the tone, humour and personality of the ad that went against the grain and resonated with an audience alienated by the slick marketing of traditional razor brands.

Its content didn't focus on technicalities or definitions of what men who shave are supposed to look or act like. Dollar Shave Club changed the conversation by talking to the customer in a completely different way. The narrator was scruffy, the backdrop was a warehouse – but the message was so strong, clear and original that it became an instant viral hit.

Dollar Shave Club was loved. But that's not the only path. If you stand for something and some people don't like it... that's OK.

The worst thing you can do is to be 'liked' by everyone. It's very rare that people who are liked by many are loved as strongly. And you can't deal with half-arsed emotions when you're a cult. You need followers fully inside or outside the circle.

It's better to have 1,000 real followers who absolutely love you and everything you do than 100,000 followers who are ambivalent.

But it's also not enough to be different and bold. You have to wear your difference with confidence.

EXAMPLE

PROTEIN WORLD

A social media storm absolutely terrifies most brands. We've seen major brand after major brand cowering to the Twitter mob in the face of some perceived offence. Whether it is deserved or not, the general direction of travel has been for brands to immediately make grovelling apologies, withdraw the advert, product or whatever the offending item was, and slink back into their hole with their tail between their legs.

In most cases, regardless of the offence, big brands believe they are protecting their brand reputation by acting this way—but they can quite easily damage their reputation among their devout followers by so quickly backtracking or cowardly succumbing to others attacking the brand. The worst thing your followers can see is you apologising for being you. Or throwing them under the bus. You're a cult leader; your followers need to feel protected, otherwise they will lose trust.

Not so with one very famous campaign from upstart brand Protein World, which built a following on the social media fallout. In the spring of 2015, huge billboard posters were displayed on the Tube featuring a slim, athletic model wearing a bikini displaying the words 'Are you beach body ready?'.

The backlash was almost immediate. The company was lambasted on social media by women's rights activists, body-positivity campaigners, eating disorder charities and others who believed the ad sent out a negative message. Some took it upon themselves to edit the Tube ads and posters by adding their own versions, which were widely shared on social media.

Yes, Protein World had succeeded in making its products go viral… but now it was time to apologise like every other brand would and say it would try harder next time.

Wasn't it?

Not a chance! If anything, the brand doubled down on its messaging.

Protein World execs got involved in rebutting some of the criticism on Twitter – even going so far as telling critics they needed to grow up. While this sent Twitter into even more of a frenzy, something interesting happened. The brand's firm rebuttal and standing up for its beliefs brought with it a stronger reaction from its customers and fans. They sided with Protein World and they did so because, as Protein World knew, they shared the same beliefs. Had Protein World capitulated to criticism, its fans would have thought differently about the brand.

Protein World was drawing a line in the sand for its followers. We stand for using protein shakes to get your body beach ready. We are different because of this. And we're not going to apologise. We're going to celebrate it. Whether you think it's wrong or right, it doesn't matter. Protein World strengthened its connection with its true fans. And to hell with the rest. They were never going to become true fans.

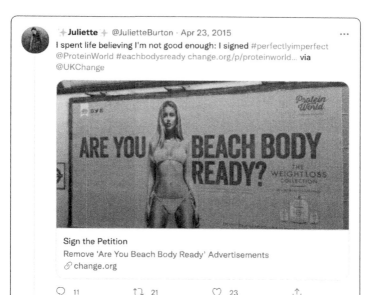

✦ **Juliette** ✦ @JulietteBurton · Apr 23, 2015   ...
I spent life believing I'm not good enough: I signed #perfectlyimperfect
@ProteinWorld #eachbodysready change.org/p/proteinworld... **via**
@UKChange

Sign the Petition
Remove 'Are You Beach Body Ready' Advertisements
𝒮 change.org

💬 11   ⟳ 21   ♡ 23   ⬆

Protein World ✔
@ProteinWorld   ...

Replying to @JulietteBurton

@JulietteBurton @UKChange why make your
insecurities our problem 😜

10:41 PM · Apr 23, 2015 · Twitter for iPhone

68 Retweets   **121** Likes

Protein World ✔
@ProteinWorld   ...

Replying to @JulietteBurton

@JulietteBurton and it's ok to be fat and out of shape
instead of healthy? We are a nation of sympathisers for
fatties #doesnthelpanyone

10:47 PM · Apr 23, 2015 · Twitter for iPhone

103 Retweets   **173** Likes

THE 'HOW TO BE DIFFERENT' CHECKLIST

Showing up in a different way doesn't need to be complicated. It can be simple. How you show up differently needs to engage more than one of the senses, including sight and sound. To get started, use this checklist:

Look different

What does your logo represent to your followers? Does it have a meaning or symbolise something important or desirable to them? This can be something as simple as choosing a bolder, more striking palette of colours to help you stand out. It may be bringing a unique personality to your visual output that feels different.

GET INVOLVED

There isn't the space or colour in this book to demonstrate this here. But you can see exact examples of how this works by signing up to the 'How to Start a Cult' mini-course. Register for free here: **www.cultbrandmethod.com**

Sound different

How do you speak to your followers? Are you a leader who colludes with, dictates to or loves your followers? Do you speak to them like Deadpool – all cheeky and knowing? Do you speak to your followers as though you're Obi-Wan and they're a young Anakin – all sage-like and caring? Your tone of voice has the power to instantly transform your relationship with your fans. Work out what is best for you.

Act different

This is all about how you act as a brand on the outside. As we've seen from the Bad Boy Running, Protein World and Dollar Shave Club examples, being passive doesn't work. You're a cult, for Chrissake – you're supposed to be making moves and taking action. The difference in the way you act serves as a focal point for your cult followers. It gains the attention of new potential cult members who see you confidently expressing your position and cult message. It strengthens the relationship with existing cult members, who feel more connected when you outwardly demonstrate confidence. And it royally pisses off all those who hate you, a side effect that emboldens your real fans even more.

Be different

This is where your cult message intersects with the delivery of the message. But there is also an operational/customer experience aspect to this which you need to take into account. (Yes, I just referred to customer experience in relation to cult followers. I told you this was a weird book.) Again, this doesn't need to be complicated. As we'll see in Chapter 11 on building belonging, how you act with your cult followers has a big impact on how they feel about you and how well they recruit and promote your CultBrand.

This is all about perception. Sure, you need to actually do it. This is a common mistake made by businesses and brands; they boast a genuine, objective difference, yet the market perceives them to be no different.

If you use the above list as a form of checklist, then you won't fall into the same trap.

HOW TO BE BOLD AND CELEBRATE YOUR DIFFERENCE

Now it's time to identify if there is a gap you can occupy so you can look, sound and act different to your competitors. We'll begin with some digging into what everyone else is doing. When we work with clients in the agency, this is the moment of truth where they usually realise how damn vanilla and boring they've been. No, I'm not forgiving it, but now you know, you know. There's no going back.

COMPETITOR AUDIT

This exercise gives you a starting point from which to work. This will highlight the most straightforward and obvious ways to be different.

- What colours are most common in the visual branding in your sector?

- How do other brands present themselves? Do they take a careful, targeted approach or do they look to be everywhere all at once?

- What do their logos look like?

- What type of language do they use?

- What tone of voice do most of them use?

What you're looking to do here is find common themes. Does everyone use the same colours? Does everyone stick to a similar palette? It may not be completely obvious until you do this exercise.

What you realise by doing an exercise like this is how little brands deviate from a common 'look'. It quickly becomes apparent that there's a serious lack of courage when it comes to standing out. This is to your advantage.

Remember, this isn't just about logos and brand colours. It's also about the language they use, features and benefits, and their tone of voice.

All the brands in your industry may have logos of different designs and colours, but do they all 'sound' the same? Do they all speak the same language? If you've not done this exercise before, it could be an eye-opener.

It's the moment you realise how samey and nondescript everyone looks to your customers.

GET INVOLVED

Want more examples of cult messaging from other brands? Sign up to the 'How to Start a Cult' mini-course. Register for free here: **www.cultbrandmethod.com**

EXERCISE

FINDING YOUR DIFFERENCE

How is your brand different from others your followers could choose?

It's time to get honest. If you're small, don't hide it. Own it. You fool no one. If you're traditional, don't deny it. Make it your advantage.

In this exercise, go through each of the points in the 'How to be different' checklist on pages 181–182 again, and highlight exactly how you are showing up.

- Look different: how are you showing up visually?

- Sound different: what makes your voice distinctive?

- Act different: how do you interact with your audience, and how do you behave compared with other businesses/brands?

- Be different: what is the perceptible, genuine difference between what you're saying and what everyone else is saying?

As a result of this exercise, you should start seeing where you can build some contrast and distance in the way you look, act and sound compared with everyone else in your market.

GET INVOLVED

Need help finding your difference? Join the Cult Leader Facebook group and get feedback on your different ideas. Go to: **www.facebook.com/groups/howtostartacult**

SUMMARY

In this chapter, you discovered that:

➤ To attract attention and win new followers, you need to be perceptibly different from anything seen before.

➤ It's not enough to be different; you need to celebrate and own your difference. Confidently. All the time.

➤ Being different is 10× more powerful than being 'better' to recruit new followers.

➤ Your CultBrand needs to show up as being different in as many ways as possible.

➤ Most marketing and branding 'experts' make differentiation into something more complicated than it needs to be.

➤ Being different can be dangerously simple – and should be, wherever possible.

➤ Leaving behind the masses and focusing on a small, committed cabal of devotees is the right path when it comes to building depth of belonging.

THE TACTICS

I n Phase 1, you spent time doing the hard preliminary work to get you to the launch phase and beyond. It's not easy stepping into becoming a cult leader. You've had to be bold, be brave and make some decisions that will feel uncomfortable.

You've worked hard, so make yourself a nice cup of tea, put your feet up and relax…

Just kidding. Like I'd suggest that! No, we're not slowing down now.

What should be clear by now is that starting and growing a cult is not a once-and-done thing. You have done the critical strategy work; now it's time to move on to tactics. This section isn't rocket science – but that doesn't mean it won't be challenging. Most people will get this far but fall by the wayside in the face of the sustained, concerted action they now need to take.

There's no hiding. The next step is hard work. Each of the four tactics in this phase needs to be baked into what you do day by day and week by week.

There is one hell of an upside, though. This is where it gets fun. This is when you see the fruits of your labour; when the cult springs to life and your followers start responding, creating and taking your brand in a direction you never thought possible.

Put on that Stetson and your sassiest chaps, saddle and up and get ready for this rodeo. It's going to be one hell of a ride.

THOU SHALT BANG THY DRUM OVER AND OVER AND OVER

"

*I've got a fever and the only prescription
is more cowbell.*

**CHRISTOPHER WALKEN ACTING AS BRUCE DICKIN-
SON, SATURDAY NIGHT LIVE**

In this chapter, I show you:

- The one activity every cult needs to do
- The ingredient you need to add to your cult message to explode awareness

- The only way to ensure you gain momentum and grow your cult following.

There's a famous *Saturday Night Live* sketch about – weirdly enough – the recording of Blue Öyster Cult's '(Don't Fear) The Reaper'.

Now, if you've heard this classic prog-rock tune, you'll know that its defining feature is the liberal use of the cowbell. It's what makes it stand out.

And it's also the butt of the joke in the sketch.

In the scene, Will Ferrell plays the obsessed cowbell-playing Gene Frenkle, whose incessant banging on said instrument is terrorising the rest of the group. They try everything to overcome the problem, including dialling it down. Finally, the advice of producer Bruce Dickinson (Christopher Walken) runs counter to the rest of the band; instead of reducing the amount of cowbell, they need to dial it up. As he insists: 'I gotta have more cowbell, baby!'

Eventually, the band relents and lets Gene go wild on the cowbell… and the rest, they say, is history.

What Bruce knew is that hammering that cowbell repeatedly and often is exactly what would make the song.

When it comes to your message, if you want to grow your following, you need to do the same: give it more cowbell.

66

Once you have a cult
message, you must
disseminate it as widely
and consistently as
possible

99

MAINTAIN MOMENTUM

This chapter is going to be like Simon Cowell – short and unsexy.

Here is the crux of the matter: once you have a cult message, you must disseminate it as widely and consistently as possible. What the leaders of cults and growing brands have in common is the need to communicate what the hell they're about, what they stand for and why they're worth listening to. This isn't a one-shot deal.

Like the mad broadcasts of a South American despot or the booming voice of Big Brother in *1984*, the regular connection between the message and the people is central to its dissemination. (I realise those are highly inappropriate examples.)

Talking of despots, if ever you need an example of this, just remember back to when Piers Morgan was in the hotseat at GMB. You only need to read the headlines the next day to see what Piers was ranting or raving about. Yes, his face is highly punchable and his bullying, hectoring approach leaves you screaming at the TV... but no one could possibly argue his message didn't get through. When he was booted for his Meghan Markle comments, the groundswell of support for his reinstatement was huge. He had a platform and he banged his drum again and again to win a legion of followers.

Consistency isn't a way – it's the *only* way

To really step into your cult leader role, you need to be persistent and consistently show up for your followers. This you cannot bypass or avoid. It cannot be short-cutted or sped up. You simply have to do it. And if you're not doing it already, you'd better start as soon as possible.

You don't run a launch campaign for your central message, shoot your load and expect the world to hear it, understand it and file it away under 'stuff we need to remember'. Hopefully, it will come as no surprise that isn't how things work.

It never fails to surprise me that organisations, businesses and brands often believe they can avoid this central tenet of the job of communication.

There is zero evidence that any other approach to spreading a message far and wide works – and particularly so in a world where everyone's conscious life is crammed with competing messages, noise and distractions.

Take the big JC. The Son of God had it all going for him when he decided to step out from behind his carpenter's bench, put down his plane and educate a heathen world on a new way of thinking and acting.

When he was walking on water or feeding the five thousand, he had the advantage that 4,999 of them weren't staring at the latest Samsung, more interested in the hottest celeb goss from

Rome or Pontius Pilate's hip new TikTok video. Jesus's message of Christian goodness needed not only his persistence, but a barrage of others to understand and carry forth his message. Thankfully, JC was a bit of a storytelling pro (and, let's be honest, a bit of a drama queen).

Tipping tables and berating whores is always a sure-fire way to get the attention of your audience. But it was the simplicity of his message and its consistent application that helped it become gospel. Let's not forget that before Christianity ruled Western civilisation, it was very much a cult.

However, a warning. What I don't advocate is reverting to the traditional, old-school way of mindless repetition to bludgeon your way into your customer's mind. You know, running the same dull ad week after week, or those irritating jingles that hit them with an unsophisticated 'buy me now' message.

These are the equivalent of that annoying song when you were a kid. The one that went: 'I know a song that will get on your nerves, get on your nerves, get on your nerves; I know a song that will get on your nerves, and it goes a bit like this… I know a song…'

You remember that song because it's painful to listen to. Yes, you remember it, but this kind of communication doesn't inspire any emotional connection or belonging. Broadcast consistently, but keep your focus on the cult message.

The constant, persistent hammer beat of your message and story being communicated week in, week out is the only way to guarantee you get into the consciousness of your audience.

The more time a follower spends with you, the stronger they feel towards your cult. That's why 12 hours of content consumed by a follower over 12 months is a stronger indicator of cult followership than 12 hours of content consumed in a week and then nothing for the remaining few months.

WHY YOU NEED TO CHOOSE THE CHANNEL

One of the most important decisions you'll make on the road to building your cult is your choice of channel. Where will you choose to promote your message?

The prevailing factor in deciding where to start broadcasting your message will hinge upon understanding who your ideal cult follower is. If you know where they are right now, then you can target them more.

In the meantime, this is the important part: no matter which platform you use to broadcast your message, you need to pick one and hammer the fuck out of it. No jumping between different media every two minutes because your 14-year-old niece has racked up 23 billion views on a new platform by dancing to 90s classics dressed as Baby Yoda. No 'trying' it for three weeks, getting no comments and storming off the platform in a huff, then spending more time telling everyone you can (on social media) how much of a waste of time social media is for getting your point across.

GET INVOLVED

Not sure about the right channel to start broadcasting your cult message? Sign up to the 'How to Start a Cult' mini-course today and explore the best options for you. Register for free here: **www.cultbrandmethod.com**

STICK WITH A CHANNEL, AND SHOW UP

Of course, that's not all you need to do. Actually taking some time to master the nuances and practices of the platform would help.

I'm all for jumping in and learning as you go. That's exactly the right thing to do. Better to get started and build your knowledge while building your following instead of waiting around for months to get everything ready. Once you have your cult message and story ready, it's time to unleash the dogs of war (or podcasting or blogging or whatever you're planning to do).

One of the key factors for the success of the BBR podcast and its cult following is the least sexy. BBR's public face is made up of the off-beat actions of the cult members, the striking merchandise and a general aura of 'We don't give a fuck'.

But the truth is that none of those elements would ever have come to fruition or reached the audience they needed to reach to gain traction without one thing: the consistent beat of the BBR message hitting the 'market' every week for three years.

The regularity and consistency of the podcast episode publication is deathly boring. Yet, unsurprisingly, it is the sole pillar around which the popularity of the podcast was born.

Maybe we could have launched a 'season' of 12 podcast episodes every year and it would still have garnered the same level of devotion. I doubt it, though.

Our journey over the hours and hours and hours of listening our devoted audience had to endure to get to this point was part of the 'indoctrination' process. There's a strange badge of honour having listened to every episode. Those who pick and choose the episodes they listen to are looked down upon. You're either all in or you're not in at all.

Now the message has taken hold and the community, the club and all the other aspects of BBR have a life of their own.

SUMMARY

In this chapter, you discovered that:

- You must spread your cult message as widely and consistently as possible.

- You cannot bypass or avoid being consistent if you want to step into your cult leader role.

- The traditional, old-school way of mindlessly repeating 'buy me now' messages no longer works.

- Choosing the right channel depends on what you are most likely to stick with.

CHAPTER 10

THOU SHALT TARGET OUTLIERS AND MISFITS

"

Well, hello Mister Fancypants. I've got news for you pal, you ain't leading but two things right now: Jack and shit... and Jack left town.

ASH, ARMY OF DARKNESS

In this chapter, I show you:

- How to pick the right audience for your cult following

- What every brand gets wrong with recruiting followers

- How to get your message in front of the right people

- How to set your followers free to recruit, promote and evangelise for you.

Bruce Campbell's Ash says, in his own inimitable way, what everyone who tries to form an army knows: you're nothing until you've got your first follower.

Every cult needs followers. People don't just follow you or your brand; they are introduced or recruited into your world. There are only two ways people enter your circle:

1. They are recruited by your followers.

2. They are recruited by your actions.

Of the two, the first is the most powerful. It's the one you're ultimately aiming to use to bring others into your cult. Recruitment by those who have been recruited themselves is more efficient and effective.

As we'll explore further in Chapter 11, recent converts are the best at converting others. Have you ever met someone who has run an Ironman Triathlon? You'll know what I mean. They'll enthuse to you how incredible it is because they've had their eyes opened to all the possibilities it brings. You can replace the word 'Ironman' for 'being a vegan', 'religious indoctrination', 'fad dieting' or anything.

However, to get things going, the second option is what you'll need to use to start your cult or form it from your existing brand or business: concerted, consistent action designed to attract and then bring the right people into your cult.

We've covered the part about bringing the right people on board from the very start. Your actions at these early stages are designed to attract the right followers and repel the wrong ones. This is a necessary step, and one that requires sustained effort until the first method of recruitment kicks in.

Recruiting the right followers is mission critical to starting and growing your cult. If you get it wrong, you bring the wrong people into the cult, weaken belonging and connection, and dramatically reduce how effectively others will recruit for you.

When you recruit the right way, you strengthen relationships within the cult, build greater connection, and motivate cult devotees to go out and do your recruiting for you.

Size isn't everything, here, either. Whether you've a few followers or thousands, target the right people and everything else gets easier.

So how do we know who to recruit, and how do we do it the right way? To answer this question, we need to understand the underlying reason why people join a cult.

"

*When you recruit the right way,
you strengthen relationships within
the cult, build greater connection,
and motivate cult devotees to go
out and do your recruiting for you*

"

GIVE THEM WHAT THEY WANT

People don't just join a cult. You don't see people wandering around nonchalantly looking for a fucking crazed-out whack job of a cult leader to follow and dedicate their life to.

People end up in a cult because something is missing and membership of a cult promises to fill that missing piece in their life. That missing piece could be anything. Love. Belonging. Companionship. Recognition. What is important is how being part of a cult allows them to become what they want to be, rather than conforming (which is often how cult membership is portrayed).

In 2008, a German film was released called *The Wave*. In the film, a history teacher is tasked with the job of helping his students get to grips with totalitarianism and manipulation to understand how the Nazis were able to take root in German society.

Like all perfectly normal, well-adjusted teachers, instead of showing a grainy video or maybe pulling a couple of examples from textbooks, he decides to set up a cult.

He sets up the students in his class to represent an autocracy. It has its own salute, its own uniform and everything. And it ends as badly as you'd expect.

(The movie's premise is based on a real-life experiment from 1971, the Stanford prison experiment, but that's a rabbit hole I'll let you go down in your own time.)

On the face of it, the film shows what happens when power and belonging take the wrong turn and become manipulation and exclusion. It's not pretty– and that's what you'd expect of the kind of cults that end with mass suicides or burning ranches surrounded by armed police.

What caught my attention was how the status of everyone within the autocracy was levelled. An autocracy was attractive to those who had been marginalised by the status quo – the misfits, the nerds, the outsiders. Once within the power structure of the community, they were given equal status to those who had a higher standing in the outside world – the jocks, the mean girls, the popular kids. It was a great leveller. For the first time, the outsiders felt heard and seen. That is the kernel to take away.

As you can see, in the wrong hands this can go south. But in the right hands, giving outsiders a voice and an opportunity to take part in a way they cannot on the 'outside' is attractive. That should be the goal of your cult: not power, not control, but the goal of belonging within the community. You allow your followers to be who they really are.

The need to be heard, the feeling that followers are being listened to, should be the primary objective for a cult. Appeal to an audience who don't currently feel heard or listened to and you will grow your cult quickly. When it comes to recruiting for your cult, the fastest route to growth is to look for people who don't get that from anywhere else.

LOOK FOR THE HOMELESS

The mistake brands make is trying to get more of the customers they already have. They look at their current customer demographic and point to it and say 'more of that'.

OK, that will certainly get you more customers. It's the 'right' and 'accepted' way to expand your customer base. Keep giving 'em what they want. It won't build you a cult, though.

To do that, you need to switch your target from people who would like to be part of your cult to those who *need* to be part of your cult.

In furtherance of this aim, consider: who needs to belong? Who is being part of your cult urgent for? Work that out and you have the key to unlocking growth.

There are communities out there for all sorts of people – but equally, there are thousands of people out there who don't feel they fit into those communities. Communities exist, but they haven't found one for themselves. Or perhaps they are trying to be part of a community but feel they don't really belong. Those are your future followers.

You see, you're looking for the homeless. You're looking to recruit those who don't feel they have a place right now.

Let's return to the example of BBR. There were already tons of serious running communities. They discussed times, speed and all the technical boring minutiae that runners like. But if you weren't bothered about time or speed, or you didn't run 40 miles a week, you probably didn't feel represented. You might have put up with being in a group like this for the lack of anything else, but you were ripe for being pulled away by something that aligned more with your reality.

That's what happened with BBR. We like running, but it doesn't rule our lives. Turns out 90% of people who run feel the same way. It's just that the conversations and communities are dominated by the keenos. So when a community came along that aligned with that 90%, removed all expectation about what a runner 'should' do and set lack of expectation as the benchmark against which to measure yourself, it met the needs of a whole section of runners who didn't fit anywhere else.

Something else made this much easier, too: we were our audience. A fast route to finding the right people is simply to look in the mirror. Look for people like you. This will also be the most authentic way of growing the cult, as you are most likely to connect with people who are like you. If you find an audience who are both currently homeless and like you, you have a strong basis for recruiting to your cult.

EXERCISE

FINDING THE HOMELESS

A useful exercise I've undertaken with many brands that wish to build a cult following is an audience audit. This involves listing all the audiences and customers you could serve.

The thing is, it may go far beyond who you are serving right now, but don't worry about that. You're not trying to figure out your next target market; you're trying to understand who *needs* you.

When you're a must-have for your audience, it's easier to recruit, bring people on board and help them. You're looking for the must-haves.

To do this exercise, set aside at least an hour and use a large blank sheet of paper or whiteboard. You're going to put down every single type of audience or customer you can possibly serve.

There's a reason it's an hour. Most people give up after a few minutes, but by dedicating a whole hour to sitting and thinking about this, you reach new depths of thought and find new audiences you didn't think of. It helps to do this with others. Again, I caveat this with the warning that you need to ensure they're on the same page when it comes to building a cult, otherwise they'll sabotage your answers.

This is step one. Step two is rating your audiences in terms of need. Rate from one to five, with one being those with the highest need and five being those with the least need.

GET INVOLVED

Want more help on how to complete the audience audit? Sign up to the 'How to Start a Cult' mini-course. Register for free here: **www.cultbrandmethod.com**

ADOPT THE RIGHT ATTITUDE TO BUILDING THE RIGHT KIND OF CULT

There's something pathetic about the way most brands conduct themselves. You see that fawning desperation in the way they try to win you over as a customer. 'Please buy stuff, please follow us, please like us.'

These brands are forever destined to remain everyman brands. They will pour more and more money into their desperate attempts to woo followers. They will morph their message to broaden their appeal. And, in time, they will end up standing for and meaning absolute zip.

The brands that survive and thrive have a much healthier attitude. They're not aloof in the idea of you becoming a fan, follower or customer. Equally, they're not desperate for you to like them, like a jilted lover desperately trying to get back with a partner who cheats on them again and again.

The leader of a CultBrand has a healthy, neutral attitude to followers. You're not going to beg people to join – you're not even going to persuade them – but when they do, they're in. The benefits of joining are self-evident; it's up to the follower to make the step. You can make clear all the benefits of being a follower, fan or customer. You just do so without caring that much whether a particular person joins or not. It can be summed up with the sentiment: 'You can join now, or you can wait. Whether you're part of it or not, this cult is going places.'

The reason for holding this attitude is about bringing the right people in at the right time. Your goal with your cult is not numbers. Leave that to the other brands that don't know better.

Your goal with your followers is depth of feeling and devotion. Everything you do from the moment they join works to strengthen their devotion and relationship with you – but they need to have presold that devotion to themselves long before they ever walk through your doors.

It's also important to remember that you're not selling. You have to take a more long-term view, and this approach forces you to do that. If you want to instantly raise the hackles of your followers, break trust and cause them to leave faster than they joined, going for the quick sale is the way to do just that. The only thing you are selling is continuing to stay within the cult.

ABQ (ALWAYS BE QUALIFYING)

Think of the recruitment process as a filter or qualification process. Don't throw an arm around as many people as possible and attempt to pull them into your sphere, like other brands. Pull out the carving knife and carefully remove those people who don't fit before they even get to the point of joining. Actively discourage people who don't feel like they'd be a good fit. If they are and they're persistent, they'll find their way in. It's about confidence.

This may come across as a cheap attempt at reverse psychology, but when you persist, you see the results. Only the most fervent, committed and engaged walk through your doors, and with them comes an energy. You must protect that energy from those less committed, who may be negative or who leave early. Don't bring lots in, only to experience lots leaving. It's demoralising for you as the cult leader and for those who are already part of your cult. Your cult members want to be surrounded by others like them, who are just as devoted to the cause. Don't let them down by letting everyone in.

EXAMPLE

DICK'S LAST RESORT

Terrible service in a restaurant or bar is pretty memorable, for all the wrong reasons. We've no problem getting straight on TripAdvisor or social media to complain about experiences that make us feel angry or frustrated. In a world where everyone expects to feel valued and to be spoken to politely, being called an asshole by your server is pretty shocking. But there's a chain of restaurants in the US that has made a name for itself for exactly that kind of rude, aggressive service – and it couldn't be more popular. Welcome to Dick's Last Resort.

In a country that prides itself on polite customer service, Dick's Last Resort is an aberration. (In the UK, we do a particular line in passive-aggressive customer service that leaves us uniquely qualified to experience this.) Pity the poor individual who walks into a Dick's Last Resort not knowing what they're getting. There's nothing special about the beer or the food; it's the backchatting, snippy serving staff who make the experience worth it. (You'll be familiar with this, of course, if you have kids.) I've been to Dick's a few times and the direct, uncompromising experience of being spoken to honestly is jaw-dropping. One member of our party asked for an ashtray only to be told, 'Thanks for the secondary smoke cancer, asshole.' By the end, you're ordering stuff just to get the staff back to the table to see what other gems they can hit you with. Dick's knows what it does. It doesn't compromise. It makes no effort to bend the experience to what you want. You can take it or leave it. And if you don't like it, they will literally tell you to fuck off. It's thrilling.

IN OR OUT? MAKE 'EM CHOOSE

Can I listen to your podcast? Can I join the group? These are questions that most brands would absolutely love to hear strangers asking. But we're not in this for vanity metrics; we're in this for belonging. You can do more damage by letting the wrong people join than you can from pretty much any other activity.

These are the two most common requests I get about BBR:

1.   Where can I listen to the podcast?

2.   How do I find the group?

To both of those, I always answer with 'I'm not sure you'd like it' or 'I'm not sure the group is for you'. For 99% of people, that is absolutely true, but most people are shocked at my response. I'm trying to actively discourage their participation.

You see, unless they've listened to a few episodes and really understand what the podcast and community are about, they're going to leave as soon as they've joined. And that, my friend, is bad. If they end up in a group that's not right for them, they are likely to be more critical, more negative and to participate less actively (or, worse, criticise those who do participate).

When someone joins your cult, you want them to already be sold. They must know it is right for them. You also need to filter out those who aren't right. You don't want people taking a chance on your cult, dipping their toes in or dabbling. That's too vague. You need to move them to a binary decision – yes, I'm in or no, it's not for me – before they join.

That's where preframing or prequalification comes in.

Preframing ensures your followers approach your cult through the right frame. We use this all the time in sales.

For example, if you're selling a premium product, you want your prospect to have a different set of buying criteria in their mind before a sales conversation, otherwise they may naturally revert to talking about price. If you preframe their conversation to heighten the value of other elements that justify a higher price, the conversation is more likely to result in a sale.

When working with brands, we first figure out what a new follower needs to know before they make a yes/no decision. Then we figure out a series of steps to get them to the point of yes/no and engineer their experience so they get there as quickly as possible.

The desperation of some brands to bring customers or followers on board as quickly as possible means they have no time for preframing. Anyone who shows any passing interest is in.

Having the wrong people associated with the cult is more damaging for existing cult followers than anything else. Harley

Davidson doesn't want stiff suits driving around on its bikes. Supreme doesn't want scruffy old guys knocking about Walmart in its Ts. Hugo Boss doesn't want its clothing to be worn by dictators and fascists... actually, scrap that last one. But the point is, you don't want your followers associating your CultBrand with someone they don't identify with. Make your future followers jump through hoops to get in.

EXERCISE

JUMPING THROUGH HOOPS

You only want followers who are good for your community. What makes a great cult follower may not be clear when you start this process, but you can build criteria around what to look for and what you don't want in future followers. As with the cult message, not only do we want to use language that attracts the right followers, but we want to repel those who aren't right.

It's a bit like looking for new customers or clients for your business. You want more of the customers who love working with you, value everything you do and make the whole experience easy and fun. And you want fewer of the pains in the ass who always argue about price, complain about everything and treat you poorly.

How do you get fewer of the second? You focus on the qualities you don't want to attract. You make a repel list.

Think about the qualities of those people you don't want in your cult. What kind of people are they? Price-sensitive? Political? Negative? Dominant?

Make a list and write down all the qualities you don't want. Now, next to each of those qualities, write a phrase that supports the reverse of that quality.

For example, what if you don't want to attract people who are price-sensitive? You can encourage them to disqualify themselves by using language like 'premium', 'high-quality', 'luxury'. They know that when they see those words, the price is likely to be high… and they don't want any of that.

Likewise, what if you don't want to attract people who are puritanical or precious? You may want to liberally use swear words in what you say.

Or what about swivel-eyed right-wing loons? Start using the language of equality or something else that sets their alarm bells ringing.

The signals you put out in your communication and broadcasts resonate with whoever is listening. Make sure you give them the opportunity to disqualify themselves.

GET INVOLVED

Unsure what to do to get your followers to jump through hoops? Head over to the Cult Leader Facebook group where you can get direct feedback and help from other cult leaders. Go to: **www.facebook.com/groups/howtostartacult**

SUMMARY

In this chapter, you discovered that:

➡ Picking the right audience is mission critical to both re-cruit new followers and strengthen the relationship and connection with existing cult members.

➡ The traditional way of winning over new fans, followers and customers may work in the short term, but it won't build you a cult.

➡ You should always prequalify future recruits to ensure they're right for the cult (and discourage those who aren't).

➡ You need future followers to make an in/out decision as quickly as possible.

➡ You need to get future followers to jump through hoops to demonstrate their dedication before joining.

THOU SHALT BUILD BELONGING

❝

My warriors, who won't take 'No' for an answer.
Who won't hang up the phone till their client
either buys or fucking dies!

JORDAN BELFORT, THE WOLF OF WALL STREET

In this chapter, I show you:

- Why building belonging is the glue that keeps a cult together

- How belonging helps you recruit more cult followers with less resistance

- What most brands get wrong about belonging (and how to avoid the same mistakes with your cult)

- The three ways to cultivate belonging and turn mere fans into devoted followers.

There's an incredibly powerful scene in the movie *The Wolf of Wall Street*, where Leonardo DiCaprio as Jordan Belfort addresses his team. After being threatened with prosecution if he doesn't step down from his role, Belfort is supposed to be saying goodbye to his troops. But his speech turns out very differently. He relives the story of the company he built and, pointing to individual team members, tells the stories of where they were and what they have become, one by one. His followers love him. They are his 'warriors'. And his rousing, chest-pounding, tear-inducing speech causes the crowd to erupt in a frenzy of celebration as he vows to protect his team and defy the prosecutors: 'The show goes on!'

The journey of his warriors has become folklore and he elevates them to heroes. Their connection and loyalty are unquestionable. This is what you're aiming for (but preferably without the money laundering and securities fraud).

This is what we've been working up to – building belonging. Belonging doesn't just emerge. You can't do everything to this point, sit back and hope your followers feel connected to a cult. The sense of belonging has to be developed and nurtured.

As humans, we seek out others to be part of a community. Regardless of whether you're the world's biggest loner or Johnny

"

*Build belonging by
lifting your followers up*

"

Popular, you have a need to belong. That need may be unsatisfied, making you feel like an outsider in your community. But a need it remains. It's so important that Maslow included it as the first psychological need in his famous hierarchy, once all the basic physical needs had been met.

This goes to the heart of why cults even exist. Pathological cults and their leaders exploit the need for belonging. That's why it's simpler to recruit those who are already feeling alienated, excluded or ignored, and why it's hard to prise away those who already have a strong sense of belonging within their social unit. Manipulative cults do it for exploitative reasons; they exploit the differences and purposely create a rift to maintain power over their followers. They use belonging as a weapon. But here's the thing: this works for a bit, but only for a bit. Time and again the love for a cult turns into fear of leaving – not a great look for your brand. Fortunately, there is another way.

Build belonging by lifting your followers up. Your devotees will love you if you help them feel good about themselves, celebrate their differences and make them feel part of something.

Unlike manipulative cults, which tell their followers they could become something more if they become part of the whole, you're telling them 'you are enough'. That is so powerful. You don't want more of them. You want them to be themselves. And that's the reason why they are part of your cult.

Building belonging is critical for the growth of your cult, both in the beginning and in the longer term.

Build belonging and you will rapidly grow your following. What you learn in this chapter will show you how to encourage your followers to recruit others – the most effective way to bring on the right kind of followers, who in turn will recruit.

Belonging also leads to increasing the momentum of the cult and making it self-sustaining.

The work you do in building belonging strengthens the cult as it seeks to reinforce the connection between its members as well as between the devotees and yourself. It really is the glue.

Enough of the benefits. There are three key ways to build belonging in your cult:

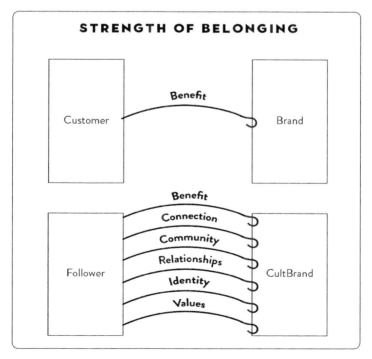

1. REWARD PARTICIPATION

There's a fact that every cult – religious, maniacal or otherwise – uses to its advantage. It's this: recent converts are the best at converting.

There is a straight line from the strength of the connection a new convert feels towards you and their desire to go forth and recruit others to your cult. Get this right and you will have others actively recruiting on your behalf.

The best way to build this strength of feeling and belonging is by persistently rewarding participation and loyalty.

For this, we want to think Pavlov and his dogs. The purpose of rewarding participation is to produce a positive feedback loop. By rewarding behaviour, you send the message that your followers are doing the right thing, and those who do the right thing get nice things. It's a positive feedback loop that encourages the kind of positive behaviour that benefits the group.

Now, when I write 'rewarding behaviour', this isn't necessarily material. If you run a business with staff, you know that money isn't always a key driver. Encouragement, recognition and acknowledgement for their contribution can be just as powerful – if not more so – than financial recompense. A reward may be something as simple as a call-out or mention for their behaviour. Public recognition for being a great example is powerful.

Following on from this, you want to identify and promote 'true believers'. Among your cult there will always be those who go a step further or are the most enthusiastic; you want to bring those people into the fold as soon as possible. The one thing that impresses me about the fans and followers of BBR who were promoted to positions of responsibility is their willingness to go above and beyond. They work for nothing, show absolute dedication and are better at promoting and recruiting than you could ever hope to achieve through sales or marketing training. They genuinely believe in the cause and will fiercely promote it because it means something powerful to them.

However, a warning: be clear that these followers have the values of the cult nailed. There is a risk that you may promote a fundamentalist or someone who has a more hard-line or warped vision of what your cult should be. The best way to identify and keep these people away from any position of visibility within the cult is to keep qualifying as they move deeper into the cult, and being clear on your prequalifying criteria to get the right followers. This is hard to get right when you start out, and it may take some time to nail.

When the wrong people end up in your cult and start acting in a way that damages the belonging, you need to act decisively. Your role is to protect your followers, and to be seen protecting them. Ultimately, you want the community to police itself, but in the short term you need to publicly call out bad behaviour and take action.

GET INVOLVED

Knowing how to take action at the right time may take time and practice. Get advice and help from other cult leaders by joining the Cult Leader Facebook group. Go to: **www.facebook.com/groups/howtostartacult**

2. STORYTELLING

There are tons of books on storytelling – why it's important and how to do it. I'm not going to tread on the toes of the authors who wrote those books here. (Check out **www.cultbrand-method.com** for a list of additional resources.) It does, however, throw up a good question: why are there so many books on storytelling?

Storytelling is as old as humanity. It's how we know stuff happened in the past, well before the advent of writing. Back before the arrival of the KFC bargain bucket, we chomped on mammoth burgers, foraged for berries and told stories around the campfire (once we'd invented fire, of course). And that's what we continued to do through ancient times... all the way up until we could put those words in a book and flog it to unsuspecting punters who are taken in by a sassy book title and the promise of a devoted following. (Sound familiar?)

The art of the story is culturally hardwired into the human psyche. It is also hardwired from a neurological perspective. There's a reason why millions tune in to watch *Coronation Street*, *EastEnders* and *Hollyoaks*. There's a reason why we need the contestants on *The X Factor* to have backstories which make us laugh or cry. And there's a reason why we get angry and vent our frustration on social media when *Game of Thrones*, *Lost*, *Dungeons & Dragons* or *Quantum Leap* don't give us the endings we hoped for. It's all because we're emotionally invested.

Your job through telling the right stories to your cult is to build that emotional investment. When your followers care about your stories, you give them a reason to come back again and again. Think like a screenwriter or author. Use the tricks of the trade.

So what stories should you tell as a cult leader? To start with, there are two places from which to draw stories:

1. The cult origin story or story of the leader (that's you, by the way).

2. The story of your followers.

The leader's story

Like brands that make the big time and grow like crazy, you need to build a narrative around how the cult started.

Into this narrative you build context, the event that triggered the birth of the cult and any adversity you may have overcome.

Mad cults build a significant narrative around the cult leader, often to the point of worship. Enough about the Bible, though. What we're doing is less about hero worship and more about inspiring others to join you.

As we're taught in school, there has to be a beginning, a middle and an end.

People get this wrong all the time. The purpose of the story is not to show you as an interesting individual. Empathy rears its cheeky little head again here; your followers may not have lived your experience, but they do need to resonate with your actions. Your origin story needs to win their attention, build rapport and act as a rallying cry to join you in your mission. The end of your story is the call to action for your followers to join you.

Your followers' stories

Just as we've promoted followers who show commitment and desire to do more, so we want to promote followers to the status of legend. We've all been part of a group where the exploits of one or two individuals have produced a story with a myth-like quality that gets repeated again and again. Those are the kinds of stories you want.

Brands that tell the stories of their customers demonstrate the devotion of their fans and outwardly signal to others 'This is what you could become'.

EXERCISE

TELL THE CULT LEADER STORY

A lot of the suggestions and actions in this chapter are predicated on your cult having started with followers in tow. Whether you have a cult already or are looking to build one from scratch, one of the key stories you need to tell is that of cult leader.

The cult leader story is the narrative that builds connection with your readers and future followers. Start by building the elements of the story– remember, we're looking for emotion and drama. The more emotive you can make your origin story, the more powerful it will be.

Here are some questions to consider so you can start building the narrative:

- How did you get into what you do now?

- When did you know this was your path?

- Were you on a different path than the one you're on now? If so, why did it change?

- Why do you do what you do?

- What is the achievement you're proudest of?

- What would you do now if you weren't doing this?

From these answers, you can start building your cult leader story.

GET INVOLVED

To see more examples of the cult leader story in action, sign up to the 'How to Start a Cult' mini-course. Register for free here: **www.cultbrandmethod.com**

---

3. PUT THINGS IN PLACE TO CONNECT

Building on rewarding participation, the cult needs to feel connection; it's not enough to just broadcast and be done with it. How do your cult followers get a piece of you? Connecting with your followers – or giving them a way of intersecting with you – is key.

Indoctrinate early

In sales and marketing terms, the best time to hit someone is when they are a hot prospect. And they are a hot prospect the moment they signal their interest. Cults work in the same way.

You have a very narrow window of opportunity when someone joins your cult or when they first choose to be part of your world. Within this window, you have the chance to turn them into a strong follower right away; miss it and your opportunity is lost.

That's why you want to indoctrinate early and as comprehensively as possible.

Here's what I mean. Firstly, when someone opts in to your email list or joins your community for the first time, you introduce yourself immediately, rapidly building trust and rapport. You want to use this opportunity to quickly build a strong relationship and connection that will serve you going forward. It's also another chance to qualify whether that person should or should not be part of your cult.

One powerful way you can do this is to personally welcome new followers and fans into your Facebook group or forum. Not just with a gif of a cat waving and a lazy mention, but actually spending time explaining, welcoming and making them feel valued. Feeling valued in the first interaction with you will go a long way.

It is also the perfect time to indoctrinate them in the cult message and the cult enemies, and demonstrate what you expect from them as part of their cult membership. Good advice: don't get weird too soon.

Do things that don't scale

When Airbnb was starting out, it was looking to expand the number of hosts outside of New York. This was tough. It struggled to gain traction. One person who knew that the success of the brand would lie in how its hosts felt about Airbnb was Paul Graham. As head of Y Combinator, the accelerator start-up of which Airbnb was part, he had seen start-ups come and go, and he knew that brands which grew a following that customers loved would survive and thrive. His specific advice was 'do things that don't scale'. In other words, do things that make your customers feel special that your (bigger) competitors can't or won't do because of their size – things like sending unexpected gifts or messages and personalised notes. The great thing about this is that if you're small, you have the advantage. You can start with just one cult follower and have an impact.

Start-ups don't just launch and grow. They go through a period where they need to aggressively recruit users. And for most start-ups, that means rolling up their sleeves and doing the right things to grow; the kind of activity that doesn't just bring followers into the fold, but delights them. You need to make them happy, make them feel stronger feelings towards you. Graham called this 'over-engagement'– treating every new user as the most important user you have.

There's another phrase from Maya Angelou that applies here. As she said: 'At the end of the day, people won't remember what you said or did, they will remember how you made them feel.'

Make your cult follower feel like they belong, and they will stick with you.

EXAMPLE

BAD BOY RUNNING

How you make this work will be particular to your cult. For BBR, we pulled this together in a very distinct way.

One of the things we did very early on with the podcast and community was to lift up listeners and followers by turning them into heroes.

I don't mean building up our guests who were already big names. Instead, this was elevating those who embodied the spirit of what we were trying to do.

If we suggested on the podcast that our listeners did something, and they did it, they'd be sure of getting mentioned in the podcast and the group. Sure, it's simple, but it's devilishly effective. We featured the stories of our followers and the odd, crazy and sometimes downright ridiculous situations they'd been in. We turned their stories into something bigger by elevating them to the status of myth and legend: such as when one of our listeners, Anja, ran the Marathon des Sables with TB, or when one of our members won a beer race without drinking any beer (he got punished, rightly, for this infringement).

Whenever we write about the podcast or are interviewed, David and I are able to repeat the key elements of the BBR story.

We connect with our audience by ensuring we have a good indoctrination sequence for new members, and we personally welcome members to the group each week. To cement our followers' loyalty, Lorna includes handwritten personal messages on the merch, berating the purchasers for buying it in the first place. Not only do followers love getting an offensive remark in the post, they love posting it online for all to see. Get this right, and you'll get a lot of funny and entertaining social media coverage.

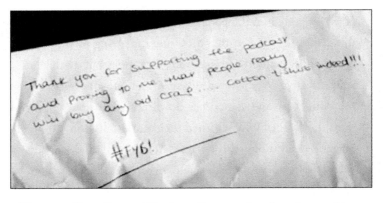

A 'love note' from Lorna: *"Thank you for supporting the podcast and proving to me that people really will buy any old crap... cotton t-shirt indeed!!!*
#FYB

GET INVOLVED

Get more advice on how to build a powerful cult leader story including a framework for telling your tale when you sign up to the 'How to Start a Cult' mini-course. Register for free here: **www.cultbrandmethod.com**

Test your cult leader story and get direct feedback by joining the Cult Leader Facebook group. Go to: **www.facebook. com/groups/howtostartacult**

SUMMARY

In this chapter, you discovered that:

- Your cult followers will love you if you help them feel good about themselves, celebrate their differences and make them feel part of something.

- Building belonging is necessary to fire up new converts to become recruiters.

- You can strengthen cult devotion by rewarding participation and promoting true believers.

- Storytelling is important to build myth and legend around your cult.

- You need to do things that others won't do to make your cult followers feel special.

THOU SHALT GIVE PLENTIFUL OPPORTUNITIES FOR THY FOLLOWERS TO DEMONSTRATE BELONGING

"

You can't force someone to fall in love with you, but you can definitely improve your odds.

YURI ORLOV, LORD OF WAR

In this chapter, I show you:

- Why it is important for cult devotees to show they are cult members, internally and externally

- How to use human tribal instincts to strengthen the relationship with your cult followers

- How to bring together people who may not have anything in common

- Why showing belonging has to be an outward expression to be really powerful.

When most couples get engaged, they're happy with the traditional method of getting down on one knee and proposing. It's traditional because it's a low threshold; anyone can buy a ring, and the act of getting down on one knee is pretty easy thanks to gravity. It's almost too easy, right?

Well, that's what Patricia Arquette thought when Nicolas Cage proposed to her minutes after they met. Instead of telling him to go away or saying 'Yes' and getting down to planning a crazy-big Hollywood wedding reception, she set Nic a series of tasks to win her hand. These tasks included procuring a black orchid, a Bob's Big Boy statue and an autograph from the famously reclusive author JD Salinger. Cage dashed off to secure all the items and got himself the date and, eventually, the answer he wanted. To get what you want, you need to be more Patricia.

Setting tasks, however difficult or strange, for your followers is a way of giving them an opportunity to show their devotion. Although I'd advise lowering the bar for your followers somewhat below the Arquette threshold, the aim should be to give plentiful opportunities for them to show they're willing to demonstrate their belonging. This could be activities and tasks, but there are other ways. We'll look at some of them right now.

At the heart of this is allowing your followers to express that: 'We want to show we belong.'

Belonging can be demonstrated through our words, how we dress and what we do. It's your job as cult leader to facilitate these options. If you left your cult followers to their own devices, they may organically organise themselves to do these things. But a better way is to consider this as you're growing your cult and to structure this demonstration of belonging for your followers.

This works because it's human instinct for us to congregate with those who we see or perceive to be the same as us. We seek commonality, and that's often through what we see in others externally. We do this in lots of ways, but the most obvious ways for groups of strangers to do so is simply being drawn to people who look, sound and act like them.

Think about football fans. By wearing a polyester shirt in certain colours, you are instantly part of a tribe. You are immediately recognised as 'friendly' and connected by others wearing the same shirt – even though you may have nothing else in common at all. You are likely to share common 'enemies' – usually a local rival or Man United. You will share the same stories of legends and, before the days of family-friendly stadia, you would likely chant the same songs. And, crucially, you will unthinkingly pay an eye-watering amount of money for the privilege of pulling on all manner of gaudy replica kit to demonstrate your belonging. It's also interesting that, among fans, there's a hierarchy of dedication that rewards the highest level of status to those hardy souls known as 'away supporters' who will happily undertake a 12-hour round trip in the middle of winter to watch their team play out a dull 0–0 draw.

I say this as a Brighton fan who supported the club through its 'homeless' days. Back then, if you wanted to watch a home game, you had to travel 150 miles there and back to Gillingham's stadium. Now Brighton is in the Premier League and its survival is no longer threatened, I still whip this out as an instant symbol of kudos among JCLs (Johnny Come Lately fans who are only supporters during the club's most successful period).

The means of showing belonging ties together everything from this book, from the cult message to the sale of merchandise. One example where this comes together in perfect cult form is with CrossFit.

EXAMPLE

CROSSFIT

There aren't many brands that fit so neatly into the cult category as CrossFit. It has all the characteristics of a cult.

Every day, CrossFit devotees head to their gym for their daily instructions. Written on the board in each gym is the WOD (Workout of the Day) which tells them what to do.

Only devotees can understand the particular lexicon of CrossFitters, mired in abbreviations such as AMRAPs, FRANs, EMOMs and RFTs.

The devotee members of the CrossFit box line up to undertake their allocated actions, pushing just that little bit harder each time under the pressure of the giant timer on the wall.

There's a clichéd adage that asks, 'How can you tell that someone does CrossFit?' 'You don't need to – they'll tell you.' Not that you'll need to be told, as they will likely be sporting official CrossFit merch from head to toe.

The one trait that demonstrates their dedication to CrossFit is their genuine evangelism about the brand and their lifestyle. They are all walking examples of their cult following, and also mouthpieces for the brand. Although it's a franchise, the real power in the CrossFit creed lies within its small communities.

But rather than a cult leader to rule them all, with the shift of the attention away from its owners who didn't exactly endear themselves during the BLM protests, the members look to the CrossFit athletes with Messiah-like devotion. If their daily attendance at the CrossFit box isn't enough for them, they can always focus on the Opens and CrossFit finals.

FOCUS ON LOW-THRESHOLD PARTICIPATION

As a cult leader, you must give followers simple and frequent opportunities to demonstrate their devotion. These three ways empower your followers to show their belonging:

1. Use the power of language

Have you ever been in court? Or an operating theatre? Or in court because of something that happened in an operating theatre?

In either of those settings, you know how quickly you can stop understanding what the hell is going on. It's because they use inclusive-exclusive language.

The language of law or medicine – or any specialist profession, for that matter – is like a fence. It keeps out those who shouldn't know, and strengthens communication between those who do.

For cult leaders, language is just as powerful. Love him or hate him, Donald Trump built a cult-like following around himself that resulted in a presidency. And his use of language was a key part of capturing the right followers' imaginations. It was child-ish, child-like and devastatingly effective. He would confer visceral, cartoonish nicknames that stuck to his opponents like glue. He would knock out catchphrases that would be chanted by his followers: 'Lock her up', 'Drain the swamp', 'Stop the steal'. If you saw a bumper sticker with one of those phrases on, you knew in a moment who you were dealing with.

Develop a lexicon of your own and deploy it to your cult.

EXERCISE

MIND YOUR LANGUAGE

When it comes to language, you can enjoy some easy wins with immediate effect. Your goal is to develop some phrasing and language that sets your brand apart, captures your followers' imagination and gets them using it. It helps if this language is visceral, emotional and memorable.

A good starting point for developing a new way of talking to your followers is by revisiting your enemies (see Chapter 7). Make a list of things that elicit an emotional response in your followers or future followers, good or bad.

Once you have this list, you want to get creative with some of the language you're using. We want nicknames and simple phrases as shorthand.

For example, a popular name for corporates or big brands is 'big, dumb companies'. Or Apple buyers are referred to as 'sheeple'. By using this language, you demonstrate whose side you're on. You're setting out your stall.

The best activity here is to go online to where your audiences are hanging out and look at the language they use to describe their pains, problems, desires and wants. You don't need to be creative and come up with language – just watch your audience carefully and they will give you all the words you need.

GET INVOLVED

Need more examples of how to deploy language as your weapon? Sign up to the 'How to Start a Cult' mini-course. Register for free here: **www.cultbrandmethod.com**

2. Identify cult devotees

There's a story reportedly told by Charlton Heston about the set of the original *Planet of the Apes* movie. The movie tells the story of a world in which apes are the dominant species and humans are simple slaves. The apes include orangutans, gorillas and chimpanzees, each of which hold different roles in primate society. The actors involved had to go through hours of make-up each day to get into character – a feat recognised by the Oscars.

Heston told the story that on set, once the actors had been through make-up and were changed, something really interesting happened. After a morning's shooting, in the lunch tent the actors in costume divided up according to their species. The orangutans ate together, the gorillas together, the chimps and the humans separately.

They didn't even realise they were doing it. It's telling that even dressed as another species, we revert back to that very human act of tribalism. Yet it's not surprising.

We know you should never judge a book by its cover. (Unless it's a Dan Brown novel, in which case you should totally judge it by its cover and avoid it.) But we innately come together with those whom we perceive to share the same characteristics.

Wearing particular clothing or items isn't just a way of connecting with others. We often wear a piece of clothing or carry an accessory to show to the world who we are. Our identity is expressed through the products and clothes we buy, use and wear.

I'm not going to talk about the Cult of Apple in this book. Too many other books, articles and (mainly fawning) blogs go into much more detail.

But I just want to talk about Apple here in relation to one of its more ridiculous actions.

A few years ago, when the iPod was released, the other innovation was the accompanying EarPod earphones. Now, everyone could know you were the proud owner of a £300+ music player... including muggers. Cue a spate of daylight robberies, and suddenly Apple was in the news for all the wrong reasons. The obvious answer was to wear normal earphones; in fact, there were calls for Apple to produce normal earphones or at least pack them with the iPod.

Apple's response was quite remarkable. They basically said 'Our users would rather be mugged than not wear Apple's earphones'. You can imagine the response.

But they were right. Apple users did continue to wear them. Being seen with Apple's distinct white EarPods was part of their identity, and no threat of a goddamn mugging was going to stop them. That is the power of visual identity.

Visual identity is a good indicator of how well your cult is growing. Followers will start to demand new ways of showing their belonging. You rarely need to push this when you're doing it right. In fact, by timing it right you allow your devotees to

"

Fundamentally, you
want your devotees to pay
to worship at the altar
of your cult

"

become inventive and find their own ways of showing their allegiance. And that means: tattoos.

If you're building a cult around a product brand, this is where your product intersects with your followers' identity.

Fundamentally, you want your devotees to pay to worship at the altar of your cult. Look, I know how sinister that sounds, but hear me out. A strong cult identity makes followers want to identify. Give them the language, tools and guidance, and they will demonstrate their belonging. By tying your product to their identity, they will effortlessly purchase from you. Not because you've coerced them or compelled them. It's because of something more powerful: you've made them feel good about themselves. And that, my friend, is the most powerful feeling you can generate in a follower.

3. Take action to show devotion

It's one thing for your cult followers to feel a sense of belonging. But to truly step into cult territory, you need to allow your followers to demonstrate their belonging.

In the movie *Fight Club*, Tyler Durden strengthens the devotion of his pseudo-militia by setting them increasingly difficult tasks. These start with the surprisingly hard 'start a fight with a stranger and lose' to planting bombs in the car parks of credit firms. It's a slippery slope from casual challenges to destroying the foundations of capitalist society. Be warned.

The thing is, it doesn't matter what the tasks are; it's the act of doing them that proves devotion. It's better to tie this in with building belonging, which we covered in the previous chapter. If you're doing a good job of storytelling and building myths and legends around your cult, you can build in activities that support these. To show you how it doesn't need to be too embarrassing or hard the first time you do it, consider what Parkrun does.

EXAMPLE

THE CHURCH OF PARKRUN

When it comes to cultish behaviour, everyone's favourite free weekly timed run is in a league of its own. Parkrun encompasses all the elements discussed in this chapter.

The popularity of Parkrun has brought with it a layer of devotion to the weekly ritual. Online communities have sprung up across the web, devoted to the event. It has almost become a religion. And with religious devotion comes dogma.

Right now, there will be a Parkrun devotee furious about the fact I've not used lowercase. (Whisper it: it's a brand name… and I don't have to follow your brand guidelines.)

When you visit a Parkrun, you see the pre-race ritual of celebrating devotion. 'Hands up if you're doing your 10th, 20th, 100th Parkrun!' Claps all round for those who are truly devoted. Not that you need to put your hand up. Most runners sport Parkrun shirts that outwardly declare their level of devotion with the milestones clear.

'Who is new?' 'Who has never done it before?' The few new ones are shepherded off to the side for a volunteer to quickly indoctrinate them in the ways of the Parkrun. For the fastest runners, they will be listening to the pre-race sermon for longer than they'll be running 5km.

BRINGING FOLLOWERS TOGETHER

Perhaps the most important element of demonstrating belonging is followers connecting with each other. Left to their own devices, your cult followers will end up wanting to meet up with or connect with other cult followers. As a cult leader, you can facilitate this by organising your own events, both online and in person.

Think about it. Cults are like a religion. And every week, if you're part of a religion, you demonstrate your belief by attending church. This regular attendance connects you with other believers as well as bringing your focus back to the creed or cult message.

In many ways, cults like Parkrun and CrossFit mirror this religious aspect. You go to the same venue or location each and every week and pray at the altar, whatever that is. The consistent dedication to regular attendance feeds your connection to the cult leader, to the message and to your fellow believers.

For some cults, you may not be able to do all of these activities to build connection. But finding ways to run events is the key to growing your following.

For example, if you were a coach or worked as a service provider, you may put on online or physical events to bring together your most devoted clients and followers. If you have a business services firm, you may organise an event around relevant topics that benefits your followers – not necessarily selling anything, but helping them. Be creative and think about what your followers would love that no one is bothering to give them.

EXAMPLE

BAD BOY RUNNING

The moment it became apparent that BBR had flipped from a mere podcast and community to a cult isn't exactly clear. Yet it was obvious that change had happened when we sold our first merchandise (probably about six months later than we should have done).

The nature of the podcast lent itself to developing our own lexicon. There were challenges – 'PB or DNF' – and bastardisations of existing language – 'Parkrace' and 'summing'. The explosion of vocabulary even led us to record an 'A to Z of Bad Boy Running' to help new followers understand what we were talking about. This epic three-part series of episodes totals around six hours of listening and is now part of the initiation for new members. If you can't survive that, you're probably not going to like the community.

The launch of the merchandise was another catalyst for growth. Finally being able to identify other Do-Badders out in the wild, as it were, precipitated more growth. It was easier to identify other followers of the cult who would connect – usually through a casual #FYB or other BBR phrase. They would share their images on social media or with the community. This would spur more people to buy merchandise, wear it out, meet up with others and start forming smaller groups they could connect with on a local or online basis.

Not everything you throw out there as a suggestion always works. But this one really did: press-ups at the finish line. I outlined the reason behind this earlier in the book as part of the BBR story (see page 29). Very quickly, it became a symbol for the community to do press-ups – sometimes halfway through a run, but more commonly at the finish line. It's a joy to watch for Do-Badders… and infuriating for organisers and other runners, which makes it all the more worthwhile. (It's enjoyable to watch conversations between runners outside the community, with one explaining to another why people do press-ups and then both moaning about their childish nature. Job done.)

Our events were also important – for those who attended, of course, but also for those who didn't but who could see that people within the cult were getting together. We ran casual runs, such as the BrewDog Run between all the BrewDog pubs in London, which was great to get on social media with everyone involved in red Ts. We also entered competitions together and organised events like the BBR Christmas party, with its now-famous 'shit' raffle. The Ultra Zone hosting at the National Running Show added another physical opportunity to meet other members of the cult and see the red merch in far greater numbers.

SETTING YOUR FOLLOWERS' CREATIVITY FREE

If you don't give your followers a means by which to show their belonging and devotion, they will invent ways to do so themselves. There is huge power in this.

In a time without races, devotion is also demonstrated with a flourishing of creativity. In addition to our official merchandise, there has been a blooming of fake merch where followers have developed their own take on the BBR brand, to hilarious effect. And instead of reaching for the 'cease and desist' like most douchebag brands, we wholeheartedly encourage it.

You see, manipulative cults (and weak brands) stifle creativity. Their culture of fear stems from an insecurity about the strength of their message. They keep everyone in line.

But cults that aren't manipulative come from a place of strength by building genuine belonging. If your connection to your followers is strong enough, you don't need to hold people back. You can let them flourish and take your brand and let them run with it.

You see this expression in so many ways of taking a brand and extending it. The strength of devotion can be seen in the sprouting of phenomena such as fan art and fan fiction, which take franchises like Disney Princesses, Harry Potter, *Game of Thrones* and *Twilight* and move them into new territory. Some franchises have seen the power of this early on. George Lucas was really smart to allow the liberal use of the Star Wars franchise by other entertainment brands such as *Family Guy* and *Robot Chicken* to take the cult brand in a new direction. The result was to strengthen the connection between followers and the original brand.

The truth is that at this stage, if you're still in the cult launch phase, it may feel you're a long way from having the numbers needed in your group to kick off these activities. But there are two important aspects to remember.

Firstly, it's a cult. You don't need huge numbers of followers to get started. As soon as you have a handful of followers, start building belonging, deepening the relationship and get them doing activities to show their devotion. It's about strength of feeling and belonging rather than numbers of followers.

The next thing to remember is that if you're doing it right and are tuned in to what your followers are saying and thinking, you'll know when to get this activity going. The best moment for these to kick in is just as it looks like there's a clamour among the followers for something to happen. For the BBR community, there were clear signals that people were looking for merchandise and were interested in meeting up more.

GET INVOLVED

Stuck for ideas and feedback on this and other cult-building exercises? Join the Facebook Cult Leaders group and see what other Cult Leaders are doing. Go to: **www.facebook.com/groups/howtostartacult**

SUMMARY

In this chapter, you discovered that:

- ➡ Tapping into human tribalism is a powerful way to give devotees the chance to show belonging.

- ➡ Giving your followers simple and straightforward ways to show belonging strengthens your relationship with them and relationships between them.

- ➡ As a cult leader, you must give followers simple and frequent opportunities to demonstrate their devotion.

- ➡ Tying your product or brand to cult identity makes it more likely that your followers will purchase your products.

THE NEXT STEP: BECOME THE CULT LEADER

O ver the last 200 or so pages, I've made the case for starting and building your own cult following.

You're either in or you're out. If I've not convinced you now, then I bid you adieu and hope you've at least gained some valuable insight from this book.

If, however, you know cult building is for you, this is just the start. I've taken you so far, but the very next step is down to you.

Every cult needs a leader. And, right now, you need to step into the cult leader role. Before you do anything else, that means committing to this path. If you have a team, it means getting buy-in for your cultish moves. (I'm sure it will come as no surprise that I recommend lavishing copies of this book upon each and every person you need to convince.)

That's it. Follow the Seven Commandments and grow your cult.

I promised you they would be simple and straightforward. They are. But simple is never the easiest path. Do not be deceived about the task ahead.

Right now, you'll be in one of two places. (There is a third, which is that you've given up on the book early. But you won't be reading this, so fuck you.)

1. You like the idea of a cult but you're not sure it's right for your brand. Or it seems a bit... well... extreme. To you, I say a big fat 'I told you so'. I expected this. Building a cult isn't for everyone. If that's you, no hard feelings. I hope you have learned something in the pages of this book to take away and use in your business.

2. You're feeling inspired and enthused. You know what a difference it will make to your brand to develop a devoted cult following. In other words, you know it's time to step up as a cult leader.

You can do it. I believe in you. But do it by the letter. Do it right. Don't try to skip what needs to be done. Because when you start building your cult and you have devoted followers, they will look to you to lead. To protect them. That means leaning into your role, not being complacent. In the words of Han Solo:

'Don't get cocky, kid.'

DID YOU SEE IT?

If you're smart, you put two and two together and saw what I was doing. Like the hoodlum Deadpool kills with a Zamboni machine, you probably saw it coming a long way off.

The strategy and tactics I show you have all been deployed in this book.

In every chapter, I've tried my hardest to get you to give up, to narrow my audience and only let those who feel committed to the cult cause slip through.

Maybe I did my job well; maybe I didn't. But if I've done my job right, you're either a staunch believer in the CultBrand method or you're here because you simply can't not finish a book you've started. Either way, welcome to the end or the beginning of your journey, depending on what you choose to do next.

HERE'S HOW YOU CAN WORK WITH ME

JOIN THE CULTBRAND PROGRAMME

You've read about the method. You've seen how brands have successfully used it to grow cult followings. Now discover how to apply it to your business or brand.

The CultBrand Programme is an immersive programme combining online lessons with coaching through each stage of the methodology. It allows you to build the foundation for your cult-building activity with direct support from coaches to help you apply the lessons to stand out, grow your following and leave your competition behind as quickly as possible.

Register for the next intake here: **www.cultbrandmethod.com**

WORK DIRECTLY WITH MY AGENCY

Every month, we start working with a small number of brands that are committed to starting and growing a cult following using the CultBrand methodology.

Discover more at **www.hellogenius.co.uk** or book a strategy call with a CultBrand coach at **www.bookmystrategy.com**

HIRE ME FOR SPEAKING OR EVENTS

Audiences love hearing about what happens when you accidentally start a cult, where it can lead and how to apply it in their own personal or professional lives. I'm available for events, either as a speaker or leading workshops to introduce and bring to life the Cult Commandments for your team or business. Discover more at **www.jodyraynsford.com** or to discuss availability, email **bookings@jodyraynsford.com**

AND A FEW
WORDS OF
THANKS

This whole book – in fact, this whole idea – started as just a headline.

I was asked to speak at a NatWest Accelerator event and had to come up with a talk that was interesting. I already knew I wanted to talk about the rise of Bad Boy Running, but it wasn't until I settled on the name of the talk – 'How to Start a Cult' – that it all fell into place. This 10-minute talk eventually turned into a one-hour workshop I presented at the Brighton Summit in 2019. And its reception was the catalyst for everything that came after.

That's why it's necessary to thank a number of people who made this possible.

For originally giving me the opportunity to speak about this, my thanks go to Olu Peyrasse and Kristina Pereckaite at the NatWest Accelerator in Brighton. It was then that the wonderful team at the Brighton Chamber – Sarah Springford, Amy

Lishman and Laura Barban— saw the value in delivering this idea to a wider audience at the Brighton Summit.

Of course, the backbone of this book is the Bad Boy Running podcast. And the podcast wouldn't exist without my co-presenter, David Hellard, whose eternal optimism and energy kept the light burning even when we thought no one was listening, and on the many occasions when I wobbled and almost wanted to quit. Also thanks to Allie Bailey, our co-host, who showed us what BBR meant beyond just the podcast and was our biggest advocate wherever she went. Special mention needs to go to Lorna Spayne, equally my biggest help and biggest troll. You wouldn't be looking at a picture of a tattoo if it wasn't for all the glorious madness of BBR superfan Amy Robson (and special thanks for her permission to use her leg as an example in these pages). Thanks also to James Mills and Dave Stuart for their press-up photos – looking good, chaps. Thanks to the indefatigible Susi Calder for generally being ace, being the adult in the room and for her image contributions. And, of course, I can't possibly forget the legion of Do-Badders, our much-loved gang of runners and non-runners in the BBR community, who bring a hilarious level of villainy and misadventure to the world of running. Thank you for all your trolling and good-natured banter.

I write for a living, so you'd think bringing a book together around something I know very well would be simple. Spoiler: it's not. That's why I'm indebted for the patience of Leila Green at Known Publishing who tirelessly nudged me through the writing process, challenging me to constantly work on being clearer in my explanations (and not randomly go off on tangents as I usually do). Also thank you to Ali Dewji at Known for his invaluable help in setting this book up in the right way to get the most amount of attention possible – one of my absolute favourite aims. Additional thanks for their advice on promoting the book go to Sapna Pieroux, Georgia Kirke and James Nicholson, who have supported me in getting the book to as many people as possible.

Also, thank you to entrepreneur-turned-coach-turned-Buddhist business coach Ben Johnson for seeing the value in developing the ideas around the cult.

And last, but certainly not least, thank you to my family, Libby, Frida and Hugo. Most authors normally write something about their long-suffering family putting up with becoming second fiddle to a book for a few months, but in all honesty, I don't think they even realised I was writing a book. They certainly do feel it, though, when I spend time working in the business and so, for their patience and their constant, unflinching love, I am forever appreciative.

Printed in Great Britain
by Amazon

41790319R00158